ENDORSEMENTS

"Urban D. has successfully created a pedagogical transformation for the believer with this book. If you change the way you see yourself, then you can change everything around you. Reframe your life and change the planet!"

KURTIS BLOW, Hip-hop Legend, Community Activist

"Tommy crushed this and gave us exactly what we needed—the right book for the right time. Perspective is everything and this book will give you a new outlook for life. Get ready, God's going to give you new vision!"

PASTOR TRAVIS HEARN, Lead Pastor at Impact Church, Phoenix Suns Chaplain, and author of *30 Days With God*

"Pastor Tommy's book 'Frames' deposits a biblical perspective on life into every reader and strengthens those that are having to stand in faith for their purpose. This book encourages us to stand on God's word, believe His promises, and know that He is with us and leading us into the plan and purpose He has for us. I believe this book will help you look out into the world through a new perspective and new frames, frames of faith, for all that God has for your life!"

MADDIE REY, Christian Recording Artist, Evangelist, and Author of *Dwell*

"Everything in life and in particular vocational ministry is in need of the proper frame of lens if one is to achieve and thrive in all that God has destined. If you can't see it, you won't believe it. If you can't see it you will fall short of the goal. If you can't see it you will bump into barriers that weren't intended for you to encounter. Pastor Tommy Kyllonen's new work is a tool that will assist with dodging dangerous detours in life, ministry and Kingdom. A needed read for every leader looking to keep their eye on the path in the race of maturing in God's work. Reframed."

REV. DR. MICHAEL CARRION, VP Church Planting and Leadership Development Redeemer City to City – NY Project

"With authenticity and passion, Tommy helps readers take an honest evaluation of the 'frames' we choose to put on each day. *Frames*, will encourage, inspire, and challenge you to reframe your perspectives and start seeing more clearly—just the way God intended!"

RANDY BEZET, Lead Pastor at Bayside Community Church

"Motivating and Interactive... this book is full of vulnerability and transparency which creates relatability. I felt inspired and empowered with the truths spoken in each chapter. I look forward to getting this book into the hands of my clients, so that they too can be encouraged by their ability to reframe their thoughts to help them thrive in their decision making!"

NATALIE SOUTHWARD, Licensed Mental Health Counselor, Founder and Director of Life Transformation Counseling

"As always Tommy makes us think differently, creatively. In his new book, he teaches us to see the world through the correct frames."

DR. DERWIN L. GRAY, Co-founder & Lead Pastor at Transformation Church and author of *How to Heal Our Racial Divide*

"In writing Frames Tommy is challenging each of us to live our lives at a totally different level by seeing every action, interaction and reaction through God's eyes and not our own. It's through God's frames that life makes sense and allows us to thrive and not just survive. If you want to thrive in your faith, Frames is a "must-read."

TRENT DUNHAM, President, Dunham+Company

"Pastor Tommy was one of my students at Southeastern University in the 90's. I have watched his ministry for the past 25 years. He started with a small group of teens and has built an awesome multi-ethnic, multi-generational, multi-class church that has networked with other churches all over the country. Tommy has a unique way of communicating with young and old. His church is a model for discipleship. His new book, Frames, is about perspectives of life and how we as Christians must reach our culture with the good news of Jesus Christ. Pastor Tommy and Crossover Church is a model for how church should be conducted in this current period of history."

GARY L. PICKENS, D.MIN, Professor, Bridges Christian College

FRAMES

YOUR FRAMES CAN **CHANGE THE GAME**

TOMMY *URBAN D.* KYLLONEN

FOREWORD BY **KEVIN *KB* BURGESS**

Tranzlation Leadership
TAMPA, FL

Tranzlation Leadership™
1235 E. Fowler Ave. Tampa, FL 33612

While all stories in this book are true, some names and identifying information may have been changed to protect the privacy of individuals.

Cover + Interior Design: Josué Marrero / Sparq Social™ (www.sparq.social)

Distributor: Publify Press / www.publifypress.com

Masterclass Filmed & Edited by Trelibra of 39 Lashes Media

ISBN: 978-1-7327782-8-3

Printed in the United States of America

www.tranzlationleadership.com/frames

This book is dedicated

to mentors that helped change my

FRAMES

Paul Kyllonen, Dennis Bingham, Joe McCutchen,

Al Palmquist, Dave Holden, Jose Barretta,

Ed Kobel, Chip Bennett, Doc Pickens,

Larry Acosta, David Charzan, Rick Warren

FRAMES

TABLE OF CONTENTS

INTRODUCTION

I love different frames. Frames for glasses come in all kinds of styles, colors, and brands. You can match them up with your outfit and make them pop, or they can be a subtle accessory, but certain frames can be expensive. They can cost you a lot financially and spiritually. It's not just about how your frames look, but more importantly, it's that they are the right match so you can see clearly through them.

Many of us are walking around with the wrong frames. They might look good on us, but the prescription for our frames is not what the Creator wrote on our script. We're not seeing a clear picture of our purpose because we're looking through the world's frames. Blurry vision can cause us to miss out on so many amazing opportunities.

The goal of this book is to help take the blinders off and correct your vision so you can see everything that God has for you. It's not just about clearly seeing the destination, but also seeing the beauty in the everyday journey as we travel there. If you keep your heart open, God can use these words to reframe your vision and open your eyes to see life differently. It can change your mind frame, heart frame, and eye frame . . . and **IF YOU CHANGE YOUR FRAMES, YOU CAN CHANGE THE GAME!**

FOREWORD

BY *KB*

We've all heard the popular dietary maxim, "You are what you eat." Whether brought to us in encouragement or passive-aggressive rebuke, the statement is true—what you consume has everything to with who you are.

Physically, if we fuel our bodies with sugar, fat, and processed foods with little to no exercise, it can literally turn our temples into disease factories. It also effects our mental and spiritual capacities. Our diets can usher in heightened anxiety, deeper depression, and depleted energy. We cannot miss the Bible's connecting spirituality to the body in its talk, gluttony, and making a god out of our stomachs. We truly **are** what we **eat**.

I believe the Bible gives a much deeper, more profound vision to who we are than even the important conversation around food. It's not "you are what you eat; it's "you are what you see." Or perhaps better stated, "what you see is who you will become." Consider these words from the Lord Jesus from

Matthew 6:23, "When your eye is unhealthy, your whole body is filled with darkness. And if the light you think you have is actually darkness, how deep that darkness is!"

Our sight, in this picture, is the most important reality in our life journey. Jesus even warns that some with "bad eyes" will be tricked into believing they are healthy, and that indeed is the worst kind of blindness.

If your vision of God, this world, and your purpose is broken, then everything else (including your diet) is at great risk. From sight flows life.

> The apostle John later writes in 1 John 3: *"See what kind of love the Father has given to us, that we should be called children of God; and so we are. The reason why the world does not know us is that it did not know Him. Beloved, we are God's children now, and what we will be has not yet appeared; but we know that when He appears we shall be like Him, because we shall SEE Him as He is."*

The more we see Jesus, the more our lives our transformed into his. Seeing is becoming. If I set my eyes on the love, character, will, and way of the Lord Jesus, I cannot help but be changed.

We have no greater task than removing the lenses of frames in which we perpetually look through that take Jesus out of focus. The goal of this book is to help take the blinders off and correct your vision so you can see everything God has for you. It's not just about clearly seeing the destination but also the beauty in the everyday journey as we travel there.

If you keep your heart open, God can use these words to reframe your vision and open your eyes to see life differently. It can change your mind frame, heart frame, and eye frame . . . and if you change your frames, you can change the game!

KEVIN *KB* BURGESS

Hip-Hop Artist, Author, Podcaster and Entrepreneur
@kb_hga | whoiskb.com

PESSIMISTIC FRAMES VS OPTIMISTIC FRAMES

RISE ABOVE THE REPORTS

Are you an optimist or pessimist? We all lean toward one or the other. Every single day, you are hit with information from all sides. The past few years, we've heard all kinds of reports about what's going on around the world, from the pandemic to politics to injustice to toilet paper shortages and much more. There have been lots of scary news. What frames are you looking through as you see and hear these reports? Your frames will help determine your decisions. Some people have thrived the past few years, while others have barely survived, and some haven't made it. Your frames can help you win and level up or take an L (loss) and miss out on some of the greatest opportunities of your life.

I want to help you rise above the reports. In Numbers 13, Moses sent out twelve scouts to go and check out the land of Canaan. His people, the Israelites, had been wandering around the wilderness for years, and they were tired. They were exhausted. They just wanted to get to the promised land.

We've all had seasons of struggling and sacrificing where we had a vision, and we were just trying to get there already. Most of us were exhausted from the pandemic . . . we just wanted it to be over already. We were desperate for a good report. The Israelites were in a spot like that. They needed a good report.

> Check out the report from the scouts in verses 25-28: *After exploring the land for forty days, the men returned to Moses, Aaron and the whole community of Israel at Kadesh in the wilderness of Paran. They reported to the whole community what they had seen and showed them the fruit they had taken from the land. This was their report to Moses: "We entered the land you sent us to explore, and it is indeed a bountiful country—a land flowing with milk and honey. Here is the kind of fruit it produces. But, the people living there are powerful, and their towns are large and fortified. We even saw giants there, the descendants of Anak!"*

The report started out good, but now it was going in the wrong direction, but in verse 30, Caleb jumped in, trying to save the situation:

> *But Caleb tried to quiet the people as they stood before Moses. "Let's go at once and take the land," he said. "We can certainly conquer it!" But the other men who had explored the land with him disagreed. "We can't go up against them! They are stronger than we are!" So they spread this bad report about the land among the Israelites.*

JUST BECAUSE YOU ARE ON THE SAME TEAM
DOESN'T MEAN YOU HAVE THE SAME FRAMES.

So you had these twelve spies go out, and they all saw the same things. They were all on the #sameteam. Just because you are on the same team doesn't mean you have the same frames. Two of them had different frames. They saw the same exact things the other ten saw, but they viewed it in a much different way. Many of you reading this book are in some type of leadership position. Leaders are going to hear and see the same reports that the people they lead are consuming, but many times, they view them much differently. That's why you are a leader! The challenge is that we now live in a world with a twenty-four-hour news cycle. There's a non-stop social media feed on Facebook, Instagram, Telegram, Tik Tok, Twitter, and YouTube. The pandemic accelerated this as we all spent even more time in front of our screens.

We all have felt overwhelmed, overstimulated, and overanxious from all this information coming at us at speeds mankind has never seen before. Each one of these platforms has a built-in algorithm that tracks everything you click on, from articles to videos to ads to purchases. It then begins to feed you more of what it thinks you would like, so you spend more time and potentially more money on that platform. This creates confirmation bias. If you have an opinion on something, it keeps feeding you more information to strengthen your opinion. This has brought even more division to our world as it has pushed people further to the left or right during the pandemic. These reports are constantly streaming through the algorithms directly to your device all day, every day. Let me ask you, what lens are you looking at those reports through? It's critical! It will shape your life, family, and ministry!

I live in Florida, and during the hurricane season, we can get some bad weather reports—fearful weather reports. The news has people locked in watching the latest storm track update to see if we are in the cone of the projected path. Some start panic buying, which causes the shelves to get emptied out at the supermarkets. Our state has lots of new people moving here. Many of those newbies are the ones that freak out the most. I've watched people board up their houses in fear, and the storm totally misses us; not even a drop of rain. Those of us who have been here for a minute take it with a grain of salt. The news is known to sensationalize just about everything to get more views so they can make more money on ads. When there are more eyes on their reports, there will be more advertisers lining up to pay a higher price. Unfortunately, the focus can be more on profit than it is on reporting the facts.

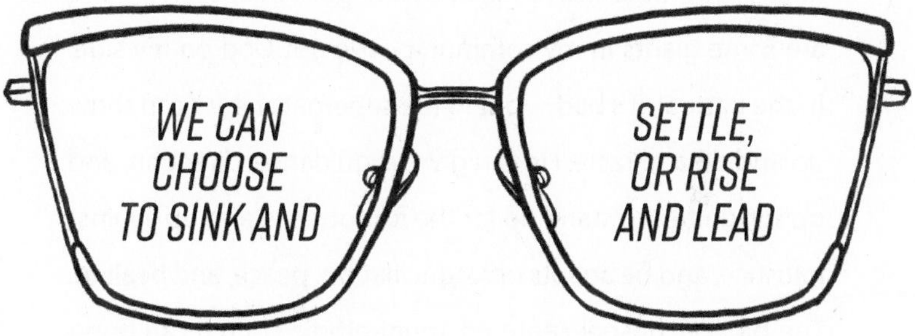
WE CAN
CHOOSE
TO SINK AND
SETTLE,
OR RISE
AND LEAD

Beyond weather reports, the past few years have been full of a variety of bad reports from Afghanistan to the border crisis to covid deaths to racism to lying politicians to corrupt corporations to rising crime to record murder rates to failing church leaders, and the list goes on. In our twenty-four-hour news cycle, it's just a constant stream of bad reports. We have to be careful because some of those reports are propaganda. Some of them have a spin on them. Some of them are fake news. On the other hand, some of the reports are solid facts. Either way, how we respond is pivotal! We can choose to sink and settle or rise and lead. It all really depends on what frames you are looking through. I watched many of those bad reports just like you, and if I look at them through natural eyes, it's discouraging. I can quickly sink and settle, but if I look at them through the frames of Christ, I can rise and lead. I can have hope and peace, even in the middle of the storm because I know God can still move and work in times like these. People need Jesus more than ever. Even if it looks bad, even if there are some giants in my community, I've got God on my side. In the natural, it's bad… but in the supernatural, he can show up and do a miracle! He can give us guidance, direction, and opportunities to stand up for the forgotten, stand up against injustice, and be agents of reconciliation, peace, and healing. The biblical, gospel-centered, multi-ethnic church can bring reconciliation, peace, and healing. Unfortunately, that is not the way most churches in American can describe themselves. The church is still one of the most segregated places in our country. So when issues of race and discrimination come up, most people don't look to the church for answers as we as a whole still don't have this right either.

I'm not here to give a bad report. I'm here to introduce some new frames to you. There is a growing tribe of gospel-centered, innovative, multi-ethnic churches that are speaking into these issues. They have an optimistic look at the problems in their communities as they are addressing them with real solutions. They are creating space for dialogue and action in their communities. This has been a difficult time for our nation and world, but I'm hopeful, and I believe this could be the church's finest hour!

MISSED OPPORTUNITIES

The Israelites just heard the report of these twelve scouts. Ten of them were bad reports, and two were good reports. So who did they go with? The bad ones! I don't think it's just because they were outnumbered; it's because human nature generally tends to be pessimistic. We're born with these frames that tend to be drawn to the negative. Check it out starting in verse 1:

> *Then the whole community began weeping aloud and they cried all night. Their voices rose in a great chorus of protest against Moses and Aaron. "If only we had died in Egypt, or even here in the wilderness!" They complained. "Why is the Lord taking us to this country only to have us die in battle? Our wives and our little ones will be carried off as plunder! Wouldn't it be better for us to return to Egypt?" Then they plotted among themselves, "Let's choose a new leader and go back to Egypt."*

Wait, what? Are you serious? You want to go back to Egypt? To slavery? If we aren't careful, we can listen to the bad reports, the wrong reports, and get in a mindset that we want to just give up on God's plan for our lives. We can want to give up on the vision he has called us to. Egypt should never be an option! Joshua and Caleb, the guys with the right frames, stepped up and said this in verse 7:

> *The land we traveled through and explored is a wonderful land! And if the Lord is pleased with us, he will bring us safely into that land and give it to us. It is a rich land flowing with milk and honey. Do not rebel against the Lord, and don't be afraid of the people of the land. They are only helpless prey to us! Don't be afraid of them!*

You would think maybe they would turn the crowd, and they would listen and go take this land that God had already promised them. Listen, when you lead higher, not everyone will want to follow or jump on the team! Some will want to kill you. Some will want to kill your dream, or at least kill your vibe. That's exactly what the people of Israel did. They were talking about stoning Joshua and Caleb! God was ready to kill all of them, but in his grace and mercy, he spared them but made a promise that not one of them would ever enter the promised land because they listened to the wrong report. Because of their disobedience, they were to wander for forty years in the wilderness. Ten people with pessimistic frames cost them forty years in the desert and no passport into the promised land!

What have you missed out on in your life because you had the wrong frames? Several years ago, a new movie theater opened up in our community, and we thought about doing some advertising for our Easter church services. We were still getting settled in our new facility, and things were financially tight. We only had a small advertising budget. I reached out to their salesperson, and he stopped by the church to talk with me. I have to admit, at the time, I had pessimistic frames on when it came to salespeople. There had recently been several people that kept calling, emailing, and stopping by to sell stuff to the church. Everyone was trying to up-sell us something that we either didn't need or couldn't afford then. It was frustrating as we were already behind on some things. So we squeezed out this small budget to possibly try something new and do some advertising on the big screens before the movie started. The sales guy started explaining that doing it for just a few weeks wouldn't statically work well, and they had plans where we could get a monthly package and do it for six months or a year. When he gave me the numbers, it was like five times the amount of what we were trying to do for these couple of weeks. I was frustrated and thought he was giving me the typical up-sell. I told him I would get back to him. That Sunday, I did something really dumb. I used the situation as an illustration. I didn't use any names or even talk about the movie theaters… so nobody knew, but he did. He was watching church online with his wife. He sent me an email and told me he and his wife loved the service and the vibe, and then came the message, which he said he enjoyed up until the part where he knew I was talking about him. He was super offended. He then went on to say that he and his wife were praying about paying for all of our advertising for the year and blessing us with that, but that was now off the table. I felt so bad. I had looked at this guy through the wrong frames. It taught me a huge lesson.

OPTIMISTIC FRAMES

On a positive note, I've had the honor the past two decades to be the lead pastor at Crossover Church in Tampa. When I stepped into that role in 2002, we only had about forty people attending on Sundays in a 200-seat auditorium. God gave me optimistic frames to envision that we would grow and need a much larger facility that would put us in a position to reach the city. I was excited and shared this crazy vision with a few leaders at the church. They didn't have the same frames as me. They diminished my vision with negative comments and lots of questions. They literally thought it was crazy, but like Michael Todd says, "It's only crazy until it happens." That year, our church attendance on Sundays doubled in size, and the next couple of years, we kept doubling and had to add a second service and then a third service. We even built an overflow patio outside with a big screen under an awning on the backside of the church. You can do that in Florida. The growth was happening! God gave us the green light in 2008 to move forward, raise money, and put our former campus up for sale. It was right in the middle of the worst economic recession in over seventy years. If we would have listened to the reports, we could have been paralyzed. If we would have listened to many voices telling us we should just wait, we wouldn't be where we are today. We chose to listen to God's voice, and we chose to rise. We saw the potential of what God could do. He opened up the doors for us to rebuild a 43,000-square-foot former Toys R' Us store. It is a crazy story full of miracles that you can read about in my book, ReBuild. Just because you choose to be optimistic doesn't mean it's gonna be easy. Just because you're obedient doesn't mean there won't be pain.

When we looked at the neighborhood around our new church facility, it could have been really easy to put on those pessimistic frames as it was mostly bad reports: high poverty, high crime, drug infestation, prostitution, homelessness, illegal immigrants, and more. This area of the city was known for its transient nature. Ninety-four percent of the housing was rental; businesses were leaving for the suburbs, and stores were closing. Our street was lined with empty storefronts and failed restaurants. It lived up to its nickname of Suitcase City.

It wasn't a good business move to come and invest millions into a building in this neighborhood. There were major giants in our hood. I'm sure there are some giants in many of your neighborhoods, just like there were some giants in the land of Canaan. Some of these things could potentially swallow us up and kill our ministry in the natural, but the people at our church saw the supernatural, and we dreamt of how the old Toys R' Us could be used for God's glory. For us, it was like a promised land flowing with milk and honey. We saw the possibilities. The problems of our neighborhood and amount of money it would take to flip the building were massive giants! But we took off our human pessimistic frames, and we decided to rise. Tell yourself ,"Decide to rise!" Write it down on a piece of paper, put it in your car or mirror, and tell yourself that each morning. Decide to rise!

Let me finish out with a good report. Don't you love good reports? I do! Over the past decade, God has helped us navigate and defeat many of these giants and rebuild so many lives. We've touched tens of thousands of people, seen thousands respond to the gospel, and over 1,600 people get baptized in the old Toys R' Us store. We've been discipling people and teaching them to serve and lead in ministry and the marketplace. God has stretched us. He has grown and matured us in so many ways. We've seen that milk and honey become a reality!

Five years after we moved into the neighborhood, it was designated as Innovation District. The government, county, city, and private businesses started working on a plan to rebuild the community. Shortly after that, I was invited to an anchor tenant meeting for a study they were doing on the community's strengths. There were about twenty of us around this big boardroom table. It was community anchors that included Busch Gardens, the research hospitals, University of South Florida, the University Mall, the University Area Community Development Corporation, the Hillsborough County School District, the Tampa Police Department... and Crossover Church. We were honored to be at the table. We were there because they heard so many good reports about us. While other churches left or sunk back and only looked inward, we decided to rise and impact our community so much that they couldn't ignore us. They knew we were a key influencer and key part of the rebuilding process. The leaders in our community formed the Tampa Innovation Partnership organization to oversee this new Innovation District.

I met the new director Mark Sharpe. He was a well-known leader in our community as he had been a county commissioner for ten years. We set up a meeting for him to come and tour our church facility. When he came here, he was blown away by our entrepreneurial spirit and all the things we were doing in the city. That day, he invited me to be on the board. He shared that the other members paid up to ten thousand dollars to be on the board, but I wouldn't have to pay anything as they needed someone like me to help them decide how we were going to spend these millions of dollars coming in to help us rebuild this community… I was like, ok—I can do that! This board has a few dozen CEO's, executives, and government officials that are decision-makers in our city. After the first year, I was voted in as a vice-chair, specifically over community engagement. Recently, I was asked to step into the role of the chairman of the board. Our church has created so many new partnerships because of our influence. The neighborhood around us now has over 1.5 billion dollars of redevelopment happening with more on the way. It's an exciting season, but we are putting parameters in place so gentrification won't push out the current residents but give them opportunities to be a part of the rebuild.

We had no idea we would be relocating our church into an up-and-coming Innovation District. We simply had the right frames on to see our community through God's eyes. Oh yeah, we have a new name now too… instead of Suitcase City, we are now rebranded as Uptown Tampa. If you would have shared this report with people a decade ago, nobody would have believed you. People thought our church was crazy to put a few million dollars into an old Toys R' Us building in the hood, but look at God! We believe the best is yet to come.

So what frames are you looking through? Remember, it can cause you to win and watch miracles happen or take a major L (loss) and miss out on some of the biggest opportunities of your life. Let's look back again at the end of this story in Numbers. Look at what the Lord told Moses and Aaron to tell the people in chapter 14, verse 29, "You will drop dead in this wilderness! Because you complained against me, everyone of you who is twenty years old or older and was included in the registration will die. You will not enter and occupy the land I swore to give to you." Wow! Because they had pessimistic frames, every single person over twenty years old would die in the wilderness and miss out on the promised land—but wait, don't miss the very last part of verse 30. It says, "The only exceptions will be Caleb and Joshua." The crowd followed the negative scouts and put on their pessimistic frames, and they all missed out, but these two guys had on their optimistic frames that anything was possible with God. We live in a culture that is listening to the bad reports. They are wearing the wrong frames. It's so easy to fit in and put on their frames, but God has called us to stand out, rock a different style, and be like Caleb and Joshua. We are called to be the exception. We'll decide to rise! We'll rise above the reports!

REFRAME IT:

1. What is a situation that you looked at through pessimistic frames, and you missed an opportunity?
2. What is a situation where you flipped it, fought the pessimistic feelings, became optimistic, and had a win?
3. After reading this chapter, what is something you are going to ReFrame in your life?

Watch The Frames Masterclass - Part 1

https://www.tranzlationleadership.com/offers/2ZMgJPF7

Use the coupon code: ***REFRAME*** to get the $99 course for Free (Create your log in and you'll be able to watch the rest of the course after each chapter.)

BLIND FRAMES VS VISION FRAMES

BLINDSPOTS

Have you ever been blinded where you weren't able to physically see? It briefly happened to me a few times, where I looked at a bright light or accidentally looked at the sun. Recently, I went and got an eye exam, and I experienced something like never before. The eye doctor put all of these different drops in my eyes, and they became super dilated. It was as close as I've come to being blinded. I literally couldn't read my phone when we finished. For a few hours, I could barely see. I had to go home, take a nap, and let my eyes rest in the dark.

Most of us take our vision for granted. We don't even think about it. We're blessed to have physical vision to see all the beauty that this world displays, but we all have blind spots. Our view gets obstructed where we can't see something that may sneak up on us. Most commonly, this happens when we're driving. I've almost been in a few accidents, but someone else in the car yelled out that something was in my blind spot. In the same way, we all have spiritual blind spots. At times, we can have blind spots with our discernment. It might be about a person or decision. We need the guidance and direction of God's Spirit to see the things missing from our view. We need relationships where trusted people have permission to call out our blind spots.

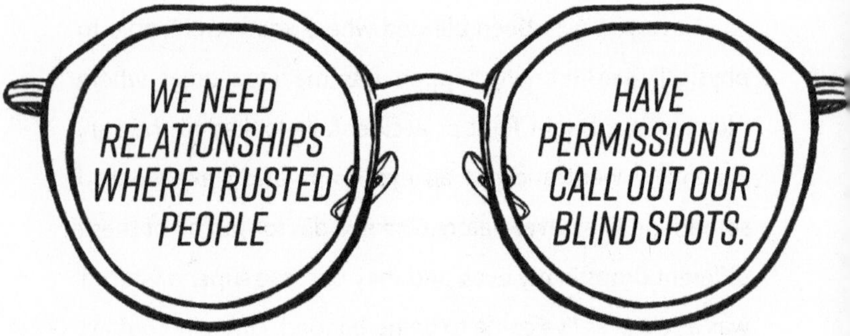
WE NEED RELATIONSHIPS WHERE TRUSTED PEOPLE
HAVE PERMISSION TO CALL OUT OUR BLIND SPOTS.

My wife has warned me about some of my blind spots. In our early years of marriage, I didn't always want to listen. Being a nationally signed artist, people were regularly coming around trying to connect with me. I'm the optimistic type and always try to see the potential in people, but back then, I was still young and naive in some ways. My wife wasn't right every time, but most of the time, she was spot on. Eventually, the blinders would be lifted off my eyes, and I would see the agendas people had and the lies they were telling. Some were trying to use me. It caused me to pay attention to my wife's wisdom and be more cautious. I still look for the potential in people, but it caused me to put up some healthy boundaries to protect my heart, family, team, and ministry.

There are many people walking around with something worse than blind spots. They are traveling through life with blind frames. They are spiritually blind to the things of God. We all know people like this; our co-workers, neighbors, friends, family, and maybe our spouse or children. It might even be you. Some people are going through life clueless about their spiritual blindness. Others had the correct frames on at one time, and eventually, the blinders crept back on. In their hearts, they know something isn't right, but they won't go back to the great physician to get an updated prescription.

Some of you desperately need to get your frames changed out as you've gone blind. Some of you aren't blind yet, but you are noticing that things are getting blurry. I went to the eye doctor because things were starting to get a little fuzzy when I was driving at night. I saw the warning signs. Don't ignore the spiritual warning signs when things start to get blurry.

When we are spiritually blind, we see the wrong things as right and the right things as wrong. Romans 1 describes people that became spiritually blind even though they knew who God was. Verse 21 says:

> *Yes, they knew God, but they wouldn't worship him as God or even give him thanks. And they began to think up foolish ideas of what God was like. As a result, their minds became dark and confused [they had blind frames on]. Claiming to be wise, they instead became utter fools. And instead of worshipping the glorious, ever-living God, they worshiped idols made to look like mere people and birds and animals and reptiles. So God abandoned them to do whatever shameful things their hearts desired. As a result, they did vile and degrading things with each other's bodies. They traded the truth about God for a lie. So they worshiped and served the things God created instead of the creator himself, who is worthy of eternal praise! Amen.*

We are living in a culture where we see these verses being lived out right in front of our eyes. People are worshiping the creation instead of the Creator. Doing the right things are considered lame and cringy, while doing the wrong things are considered cool and celebrated. Cancel culture has caused many people to fall back and stay quiet about what they believe. They're afraid they will be called out and lose some of their position, power, influence, and money.

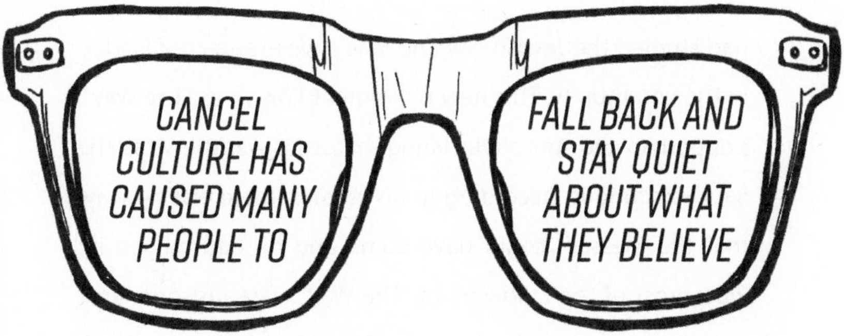

CANCEL CULTURE HAS CAUSED MANY PEOPLE TO
FALL BACK AND STAY QUIET ABOUT WHAT THEY BELIEVE

They say money changes you. I believe it, but it doesn't have to be a negative change. I've seen people that were faithful and generous when they only had minimal resources. God began to bless them, and because they had the right frames on, they were able to take care of their family in better ways and, at the same time, become even more generous. On the other hand, I've seen money blind other people. They couldn't handle it. I know people that have literally changed their names, style, friends, and become totally different. Blind frames are expensive, and they can cost you your spouse, sanity and even salvation.

BLIND AND YOU DON'T KNOW IT

The scary thing about blind frames is that many people don't even know they are rocking them. In fact, some of them believe they are exactly where they are supposed to be. An example from Scripture is Saul. He was a religious leader that was passionately persecuting Christians. Saul had studied the Jewish law and was a well-respected leader in the community. This new movement known as "The Way" popped up and started declaring that Jesus was the Messiah. Saul was furious. According to his studies, there was no way that the Messiah could have come and he had missed it. Plus, most of the followers of "The Way" were just ordinary, poor, and working-class people. They weren't the educated scholarly type that Saul normally associated with. He was spiritually blind, so he fought against the followers of Jesus.

In Acts 7, we see Stephen step up and represent Jesus and share the gospel with the religious council. He was trying to take the blind frames off of his fellow Jews, but in the end, they dragged him out of the city, and they stoned him to death. Saul was right there in the mix, applauding the murder of Stephen. Acts 8:1 says:

> *Saul was one of the witnesses, and he agreed completely with the killing of Stephen. A great wave of persecution began that day, sweeping over the church in Jerusalem; and all the believers except the apostles were scattered through the regions of Judea and Samaria. (Some devout men came and buried Stephen with great mourning.) But Saul was going everywhere to destroy the church. He went from house to house, dragging out both men and women to throw them into prison.*

Saul thought he was doing the right thing. He was defending the Jewish faith and the laws he studied for so many years. Saul was sincere, but he was sincerely wrong! As he went around the city arresting Christians, he found out many of them were scattering to other places. He went to the high priest and got arrest warrants to go to local cities to catch up with them, arrest them, and throw them in jail. He was determined to stamp out this movement that was promoting Jesus. Then the unexpected happened. His blind frames were removed. In Acts 9:3, it says:

> *As he was approaching Damascus on this mission, a light from heaven suddenly shone down around him. He fell to the ground and heard a voice saying to him, "Saul! Saul! Why are you persecuting me?" "Who are you, Lord?" Saul asked. And the voice replied, "I am Jesus, the one you are persecuting! Now get up and go into the city, and you will be told what you must do." The men with Saul stood speechless, for they heard the sound of someone's voice but saw no*

one! Saul picked himself up off the ground, but when he opened his eyes he was BLIND. So his companions led him by the hand to Damascus He remained there blind for three days and did not eat or drink (emphasis mine).

I can only imagine what a confusing moment that was for Saul. He had believed this stuff about Jesus was just another false religion popping up that he had to stop. It was his duty as a good religious leader to put an end to it. Here he was on this mission to go against the followers of Jesus, and suddenly he gets stopped in his tracks by Jesus himself. Remember, Jesus had already died, resurrected, and ascended into heaven. He came back to have a face-to-face meeting with Saul. In that moment, Saul was physically blinded, but his spiritual blind frames were removed. He realized he had been playing for the wrong team. All the training, classes, studying, and school loans that Saul had worked so hard for to become a rising religious leader… it wasn't truth.

Have you ever had an epiphany where the blind frames were lifted, and you realized you were lied to? Have you ever got scammed? When I first got into ministry in the nineties, there was an older guy in my church that signed me up to be in this vitamin company. He was making several thousand dollars a week. That was a lot of money to me back in 1997! He was gassing up my head that God was going to provide for my family through this because I was sacrificing and doing urban ministry. I went to a couple of those multi-level-marking meetings they had in a hotel ballroom where they motivate everyone to sign other people up. I had been an athlete, so staying healthy was important to me. I thought this was a good thing that could help other people and create a stream of income for my family as I did ministry with very little pay.

I tried my hardest to get everyone I knew to come to these vitamin meetings. Nobody was really interested, and I got frustrated.

They had this big celebrity that was about to launch these TV commercials nationally, and everyone who signed up would automatically be put in our downlines. We were told we would make commission off of them. This was the time to get in! This was the ground floor. We could all be making thousands of dollars every week of residual vitamin money. I got blinded by all the rah-rah. I thought this was it! In the end, the celebrity endorser backed out, and I was stuck with a bunch of overpriced vitamins. The blinders were lifted, and I switched teams. I'm all about vitamins but not about getting them from an overpriced multi-level-marketing program. I warn people to stay away from those things.

It's ironic that Saul was spiritually blinded and those frames were smashed, but now he was physically blinded. We know his spiritual blinders were being lifted because we see that Jesus told Ananias about Saul and said, "He is praying to me right now." Saul was praying to Jesus! The guy that was on a mission to arrest people for preaching about Jesus was now praying to him! Even though he was physically blinded, God began showing Saul something in the spirit realm. Saul saw a vision of a man named Ananias come in and lay hands on him so he could physically see again.

The funny thing is that when Jesus was telling Ananias about this, Ananias was hesitant. He heard about the reputation that Saul had. Saul was going around arresting Christians and persecuting them. Ananias was worried he might get thrown in jail, but Jesus assured him and said in verse 15, "Go, for Saul is my chosen instrument to take my message to the Gentiles and to kings, as well as the people of Israel. And I will show him how much he must suffer for my name's sake." So what did Ananias do? Check out verses 17-18:

> *So Ananias went and found Saul. He laid hands on him and said, "Brother Saul, the Lord Jesus, who appeared to you on the road, has sent me so that you might regain your sight and be filled with the Holy Spirit." Instantly something like scales fell from Saul's eyes, and he regained his sight. Then he got up and was baptized.*

SWITCHING TEAMS

Saul switched teams. His blind frames were lifted. He was now seeing clearly! He had a new pair of vision frames. The Scripture says that he immediately started preaching about Jesus and telling people he was the Son of God. Like Ananias, there were many Christians that were very hesitant with Saul at first. Some of them thought it might be a trap. Maybe Saul was just acting like he believed to get a bunch of Christians together and then round them up and take them to jail. There were also some that had friends and family arrested by Saul. Many of the disciples were friends with Stephen who was stoned to death as Saul watched and cheered. So you can imagine there were all kinds of emotions around this conversion of Saul switching teams, but soon they saw it was real, and they began to trust him and include him.

When I first fully switched teams and started following Jesus, I had some friends that weren't sure if I was being real. I had some friends that were saying I would be back at the club with them soon. There was another friend of mine that I used to regularly shoplift with, and he was taunting me that I would be partnering back up with him as soon as I wanted some new clothes. There is a series on Apple TV called See. It's in a futuristic setting where everyone is born blind. It had been like that for hundreds of years, but suddenly some people were being born with vision. They were actually considered evil and were called witches. They were hunted by "witch finders," who had a mission to kill them as vision was forbidden. They wanted everyone to stay blind. The irony in our world today is that people with the ability to spiritually see are often labeled as the evil ones. I believe that will increase in the days to come as more and more people will have blind frames. I felt some of that judgment from my non-Christian friends. They wanted me to stay blind and had no desire to see what I was seeing. On the other hand, I had Christian friends that knew I hadn't been living right, and they were closely watching me as they didn't fully trust my conversion at first. When your blind frames are lifted and you start fully following Jesus, there will be people that might doubt or even make fun of you. That's okay. It's usually part of the journey. Stay consistent. Stay faithful. They will eventually see you are rocking different frames.

The beautiful thing is when the blind frames are gone, the sky is the limit. You can now begin to see God's plan for your life. This was an exciting season for me. I didn't immediately see my purpose, but as I was seeking, I was getting more and more glimpses. Soon, it was clear what I was called to do. I had a new vision. I knew I was called to urban ministry, leading a diverse ministry in the city using my music and creativity. I was all in. I didn't exactly know what it would look like, but I transitioned and went to Southeastern University and moved from PA to FL.

FRAMES ARE CONTAGIOUS

Just because you shed your blind frames doesn't mean they can't creep back on. I moved to Florida to leave behind some of my friends and bad influences in Philly. I came down south with fresh vision, but I quickly got blinded by this new, exciting environment. Within the first month, I found myself doing the same stuff that I was struggling with up north. I was just in a different city with different people. My heart was still vulnerable, and I was spiritually weak. A new environment can be a great benefit, but you have to guard your heart in the transition, or your vision can start to get blurry again. One of my key problems was that I started hanging out with people rocking blind frames. Many of them had no spiritual purpose or direction. Blind frames can be contagious. Be careful who you spend your quality time with. My mom used to have this saying that I literally despised, but now as a parent, I can see there was so much wisdom in it. I now say it to my kids, and they roll their eyes at me. I'm passing it on to you as advice too. I hope you're not rolling your eyes at me. My mom used to say, "Show me your friends, and I'll show you your future." If you always hang around spiritually blind people, you might catch cataracts.

I had to intentionally stop hanging out with certain people and build some new friendships and habits. This actually wasn't that hard because two major things happened in that season. I got a job working as a server at a restaurant several nights a week, and I started dating a solid Christian girl. My schedule filled up with some positive things. I was busy working to pay off my school bill and building a relationship with this amazing girl named Lucy (who I have now been married to for over twenty-five years!). Here's some good news; if you have blind frames and start hanging around with people who can clearly see, it can also be contagious. I chose to put myself around the right people and environments that would help me spiritually grow and give me new vision. I put up new boundaries and was brutally honest about my weaknesses. My roommate, my girlfriend, and some of my other friends held me accountable and encouraged me in my growth.

The blurriness faded, and my spiritual vision became super focused. I watched God use me, provide for me, and give me direction for my uncertain future. My reputation switched from being this immature guy to becoming a leader on campus.

Saul's reputation also began to change up. In fact, it looks like he got a name change from Saul to Paul. This is commonly taught that Jesus changed his name when he had his encounter with him on the road to Damascus that we just read about. That sounds like a great part of the story… his blinders got taken off, and he got a new name. I hate to spoil the fun, but if you do your research, that's not exactly how it went down. The name Saul came from the famous first king of Israel, from the tribe of Benjamin, to which Saul belonged. It simply is his Hebrew name. Paul is his Greek name, derived from the Latin surname Paulus. Many immigrants to English-speaking countries take an Anglicized name on top of their ethnic name. Many Greek-speaking Jews in Paul's day would have a Jewish/Hebrew name and Hellenistic/Greek name. My grandfather Efthemios Demetrios Givas immigrated from Greece to America and took on the American name Thomas. That's where I get my name from. When Saul/Paul launches his Gentile-focused ministry among primarily Greek speakers (starting in Acts 13:9), it's natural for Luke, the author of Acts, to begin referring exclusively to Saul by his Greek name Paul.

When your blind frames are removed and you start living for God, he begins to use you in ways you never dreamt or imagined. I know that some of you reading this might be thinking, "God could never use me in big ways because I've messed up in some major areas." Wait, what? Did you catch what just happened with Saul/Paul? Let me recap; he went from a Christian persecutor to a Christian preacher. He went from taking people's lives to giving people new life in Christ. This guy who was known for arresting and killing Christians went on to write the majority of the New Testament. So if you think God can't use you, just look at Saul/Paul. God gave him this calling to go and share the gospel of Jesus with Gentiles (people that weren't Jewish). Saul was a Jewish religious leader that had studied for years to spiritually lead his people. He was a rising star in this circle. Now his blind frames are crushed and God gives him this new mission to reach a totally different people group. He connects with the multi-ethnic church at Antioch, and they send him out on these missionary journeys to start new churches in Gentile cities. God used Paul in amazing ways to start faith communities all over the Roman Empire. When you can spiritually see, it becomes an exciting journey each day. God gives you new vision frames. We can now begin to see people and situations the way that our Creator sees them. He puts people in our paths and regularly gives us new missions to accomplish for him.

I'm passionate to help people remove their blind frames. Since my blind frames were removed back in the day, I've been on the grind to help others clearly see in the urban community. It hasn't been easy. In the urban community, the needs are higher, and the resources are lower. Paul made tents to support his missions work (his side hustle was literally being a tentmaker). I rapped. I could have gone and gotten a job waiting tables at a restaurant (like I did in college), or I could have gotten my barber license (I also did this in high school and college). Instead, God led me to do my music to spread his Word and support my family. I wasn't sure that would create a steady income, but by God's grace, it did. After a few years, I got signed to a national label and started touring around the country and overseas. It expanded my ability to help so many people remove their blind frames. It gave me a new expanded vision of what God wanted me to do at home at Crossover Church. It created the launching pad for our church to become a teaching church. God was using our church in new innovative ways, and we wanted to train other churches on how they could be more effective in their communities. In the year 2000, we launched our Flavor Fest Urban Leadership Conference, which has now trained over 5,000 leaders over the past two decades (www.flavorfest.org). We are multiplying our mission of removing blind frames for people in cities all over the world.

I grew up lower-income and didn't get to travel much. Family vacations were going to my grandparents' house about an hour away. I never got on a plane until I was twenty years old. It's ironic that earlier that same year, my blind frames were lifted. God began to open doors that I never would have dreamt or imagined. Now, I'm on a couple of planes every month traveling to speak, preach, teach, do music, and help people remove their blind frames. I never would have dreamed that I would be creating albums, writing books, training leaders, and even ministering to some of my hip-hop heroes that I grew up listening to. It's an exciting journey when you take off the blind frames and get some vision frames.

REFRAME IT

1. What are some of your blind spots?
2. Have you ever had blind lenses on, and they were lifted, and you literally switched teams about something in your life?
3. What was your experience like when your spiritual blinders were lifted, and you saw Jesus as your savior?

Watch the Frames Masterclass - Part 2
Log in at *www.tranzlationleadership.com*
and the course will be in your library if you followed the directions at the end of chapter 1.

3

TAINTED FRAMES VS CLEAN FRAMES

MO' MONEY MO' PROBLEMS

Success can taint our vision. Resources can blur our vision. Self-sufficiency can muddy up our vision, but wait... those are things that everyone seems to be striving for. I know. We all would like to be successful in life. We all would like to be self-sufficient with plenty of resources. Those things aren't bad. In fact, I'm in pursuit of those things myself, but there is tension. If we don't stay focused along the journey, the very things we worked so hard for can be the very things that cause our fall. If we aren't careful, these amazing accomplishments can actually taint our vision and wreck our lives.

I've been in and around the music industry for over two decades. I've shared the stage and built close relationships with many talented artists. I watched some of these artists go from nobody knowing them to millions knowing them. Every single one that had that type of success had some serious struggles adjusting to that new normal. Some of them grew through it due to accountability, counseling, and the support of their local church. Others ended up losing their marriages, dreams, and careers. Some even walked away from the very faith they sang and rapped about. My heart breaks when I reflect on how some of my friends' frames became so tainted.

King Solomon asked for wisdom, and God blessed him with it. His frames were clean! He was laser-focused, but his incredible wisdom caused his success and resources to skyrocket. He literally became the richest man to ever live on this planet. Wealthresult.com and several other historical research has his peak wealth estimated over $2 Trillion dollars in today's economics. This guy had everything that their civilization had to offer. His kingdom prospered under his leadership. This guy was the man. Everyone wanted to be around him and learn from him. He wasn't just a rich leader; he was a cool leader with huge popularity. MC Solomon was also an artist that wrote poetry and created thousands of songs. Solomon had number-one hits being sung all over the kingdom. When you get on that level, it can become hard to balance. Solomon had 700 wives and 300 concubines. Imagine trying to balance all of that estrogen! As all of this grew, his frames became more and more tainted. Toward the end of his life, he wrote the book of Ecclesiastes. It is one of the most depressing books in the Bible. This guy had everything you could dream of, every luxury and pleasure available to man. He said in Chapter 2, starting in verse 9:

So I became greater than all who had lived in Jerusalem before me, and my wisdom never failed me. Anything I wanted, I would take. I denied myself no pleasure. I even found great pleasure in hard work, a reward for all my labors. But as I looked at everything I had worked so hard to accomplish, it was all so meaningless—like chasing the wind. There was nothing really worthwhile anywhere.

Wow… pretty sad, right? He was living the lifestyle of the rich and famous, and he was empty. As his success grew, his frames got blurrier and blurrier, and he grew further and further away from God.

We notice when there is a quick change in our vision. If our frames get some smudges on them, we'll stop and clean them. If we're in Florida in some air conditioning, and we walk outside into the heat, the humidity can fog up our frames. We immediately wipe them off, but tainted frames happen slowly over time. The residue of our hustle can slowly build up. Our eyes gradually adjust to the subtle changes in our attitude, standards, and motives. We might not even notice, and if we do, we'll tell ourselves we're moving the line on those things slightly so we can reach our goals faster. It's like the old story about the frog in a pot of water. If you put a frog in a boiling pot of water, he will immediately jump out. If you put him in a pot of room temperature water and slowly turn up the heat until it boils, the frog will boil to death. It won't jump out because the change is slow and steady. That is how so many people with tainted frames destroy their lives, little by little.

OUR UNEXPECTED 2020 VISION

The pandemic forced all of us to make some rapid changes when it first started. At the beginning of 2020, nobody saw it coming. All of us were making plans for this amazing new year and decade. Some called it the roaring 20s. Everybody was on that 2020 vision.

I remember following the news about this new virus in China. Most of us thought it would never affect us over here, but in January, it actually started affecting me and got me wondering. I ordered some supplies from China, and my contact texted me that he could no longer leave his house due to a mandated lockdown. My order was on hold indefinitely. I had lunch with a brother from my church and told him about it, and I said, "Imagine if that happened here; we wouldn't be able to have church in person. We would have to stream it online only. Wouldn't that be crazy?" We both laughed as we "knew" that would never actually happen. Six weeks later, it did.

Many people still had clean vision at first, but the effects of the pandemic started to taint our views as it dragged on and on. In the beginning, we were told it would only take thirty days to "flatten the curve." We all hoped that things would quickly go back to normal, but as months and months went by, we realized a new normal was emerging. Some things would never be the same. In the process of the pandemic, many people's vision gradually got more and more blurry. The protocols of us staying at home, social distancing, and wearing masks were a huge disruption in our social interaction.

We were designed for community, and that was mostly restricted to virtual interaction for a season. All of us had a major increase in screen time. We went to work online, went to school online, went to the doctor online, shopped online, went to church online, and much more, but many of us spent even more recreational time online. We watched more Netflix and spent more time on social media. This amount especially skyrocketed among teenagers. USA Today reported that teenagers' recreational screen time went from 3.8 hours a day to 7.7 hours a day. That was in addition to them being online for school for five to seven hours daily. The article stated, "As screen time increased, so did adolescents' worry and stress, while their coping abilities declined. Previous studies have linked high screen time with poor mental health. Excessive screen time has not only been linked to poor mental health, but also poor physical health." [1]

Another study said: The World Health Organization highlighted that increased screen time replaces healthy behaviors and habits like physical activity and sleep routine, and leads to potentially harmful effects such as reduced sleep or day-night reversal, headaches, neck pain, myopia, digital eye syndrome and cardiovascular risk factors such as obesity, high blood pressure, and insulin resistance due to increased sedentary time among adults. [2]

As a pastor, I watched people's frames get more and more tainted as the pandemic continued. As a coach of pastors, I watched many leaders get more and more discouraged. As a father with two teenagers, I watched it happen at home as well. New habits were formed. Many of them weren't good ones. As a result, depression, anxiety, alcoholism, drug use, and overdose deaths all went through the roof. My friend who is a counselor is overwhelmed with clients. He is working twelve hours a day with a waiting list for months. Another friend who runs a counseling center has doubled the amount of counselors and had to move to a larger space due to all the new demand.

---

[1] Adrianna Rodriguez, "Screen time among teenagers during COVID more than doubled outside of virtual school, study finds" www.usatoday.com - Nov. 1st, 2021.

[2] Apurvakumar Pandya and Pragya Lodha, "Social connectedness, excessive screen time during COVID-19 and Mental Health: A review of current evidence. - www.frontiersin.org - July 21, 2021.

MANY PEOPLE HAVE DEVELOPED
TAINTED FRAMES DURING THE PANDEMIC

People have created new rhythms in their lives, but many of them are not in rhythm with their Creator. Two years into the pandemic, church attendance has still not came back to pre-pandemic levels. There are some people that have legit health issues and restrictions, but most people are going out everywhere except back to church. They say they are not comfortable coming back to church with all the people, but you see them on social media at packed sporting events, concerts, parties, and restaurants. Sometimes it seems like church is the only place covid still exists. Okay, I'm venting a little bit as a pastor. My point is that many people have developed tainted frames during the pandemic.

A NEW PRESCRIPTION

The people in the ancient city of Laodicea also went through a major crisis. It wasn't a pandemic; it was an earthquake. The people of Laodicea were very independent, much like Americans. Their city was prosperous due to their booming textile industry. They had this designer Gucci black wool that everyone loved. The Laodiceans were killing it.

When the earthquake hit around AD 60, it devastated their city. The Roman government offered them help, but they refused it. They actually refused a government bailout and stimulus checks (that part wasn't like Americans). Wait, what? Why? Because the Laodiceans were prideful and insisted on using their own resources to rebuild. They rebuilt, and things were soon stronger than ever. This boosted their "we got this" mentality to even greater heights. In Revelation 3, they are accused of being lukewarm. So many people take that scripture out of context. I won't get into that as I broke that down in my Love Our City book.

Right after the lukewarm accusation, it says in verse 17, "You say, 'I am rich. I have everything I want. I don't need a thing!' And you don't realize that you are wretched and miserable and poor and blind and naked." Wow, they had the attitude that they could pull it off on their own. They thought they were all good, and God came along and dropped the truth bomb on them that they were not righteous; they were ratchet! Jesus then gave the Laodiceans a new prescription to go from self-reliance to total dependence on God, to go from tainted frames to clean frames. Jesus instructed them to buy three things. They couldn't get this on Amazon Prime or at the bougie Beverly Hills mall of Laodicea. Watch what happened next: "So I advise you to buy gold from me—gold that has been purified by fire. Then you will be rich. Also buy white garments from me so that you will not be shamed by your nakedness, and ointment for your eyes so you will be able to see."

Laodicea was one of the richest cities in ancient history. Many people could afford to buy whatever they wanted, but here God was saying they needed spiritual riches through faith in Christ. He mentioned gold that had been purified by fire. Earthly riches will burn up, but spiritual wealth has eternal value. There is also irony in the white garments. The Laodiceans were famous for their black wool. God was saying that their luxurious black wool didn't spiritually cover them. They needed to get some of my off-white garments (some of ya'll will get that) that would really cover you. Then that last part about the ointment for their eyes hit different because he called them blind. They were blind because their frames became so tainted from their own wealth.

Their prosperity in the city was also due to their well-known eye ointment. People came from all over the Roman Empire to get treated at their famous eye clinic and school. Jesus was saying that his prescription spiritual eye ointment would help them clear up their tainted frames. He was claiming it was much better than their over-the-counter eye ointment.

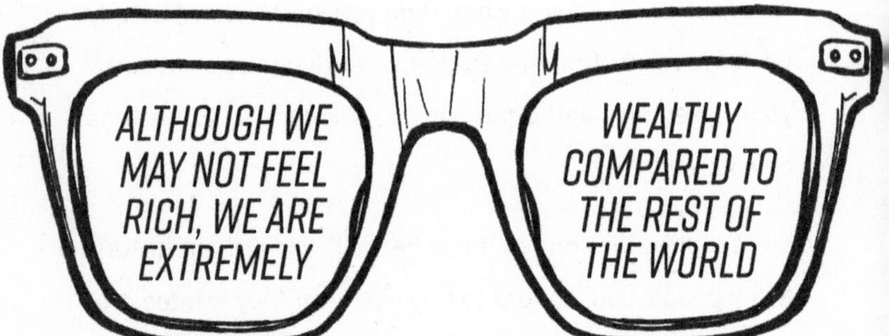

Even though thousands of years and miles separate us from the Laodiceans, we have a lot more in common with them than we think. Most of us have access to buy all kinds of stuff right from our phones. Because of their wealth, the

Laodiceans could have whatever luxuries they desired. Although we may not feel rich, we are extremely wealthy compared to the rest of the world, but the material things we purchase will soon get old, worn out, and eventually go out of style. Material things can be a blessing from God, but when we put our priorities on the created instead of the Creator, that's when the frames start fogging up.

FOGGED-UP FAITH

The pandemic of covid definitely fogged up some frames, but in addition, the pandemic of injustice added a thick layer of haze for many. Racial injustice has always been around, but it started to bubble up to the surface once we had social media to greater expose it. The Trayvon Martin case was one of the first big ones to gain traction. Eventually, this led to actual filming of several incidents of unarmed black men being killed by police officers. In many cases, the officers were acquitted, and the tension kept building in urban communities around the country. We felt it in Tampa and addressed it several times at our church. We had conversations with community leaders, residents, police officers, and government officials. We were grateful to be a safe place to have authentic dialogue and push for reform, reconciliation, and healing.

Then the pandemic hit, and we were all on lockdown for

several months. Many people lost their jobs, businesses, loved ones, and some lost their minds. It was a challenging season like nothing we had ever experienced. We were just starting to come back outside with things slowly reopening, and it seemed like it was the perfect storm. People were frustrated, isolated, and spending way too much screen time at home. On May 25, 2020, the murder of George Floyd was streamed live to millions of phones around the world. It was horrifying. It was a turning point in many ways. For some, it became the moment they finally realized there was a problem. For some, they finally began to speak up to use their platforms to speak out against racial injustice, but for many, it was a tipping-point moment of enough being enough. It sparked protests around the world in cities everywhere. Many of these protests were peaceful and stood for justice and reform, but with so much pent-up frustration layered on from the pandemic, it became an excuse for some people to wild out and get violent. Nearly every major US city had protests that ended in looting and destruction. It was like nothing I've ever seen in my lifetime.

The epicenter of the looting in Tampa was on Fowler Avenue on the very street that my church is located. It's a major artery that over 65,000 cars travel on eight lanes each day. Over forty businesses were looted and several burned to the ground.

It was heartbreaking to watch our community get destroyed. At the time, our church was doing a grocery drive-thru every Friday in our parking lot. In addition to groceries, we gave out hot meals to hundreds of families each week. We purchased those hot meals from a local Vietnamese restaurant so we could help them stay in business. We picked up meals from them that Friday, and the next day, their business was torched. Thank God our church was untouched, but our neighbors to the west and across the street were both looted. They lost tens of thousands of dollars of stolen merchandise. Our neighborhood looked like a war zone with businesses boarded up for blocks and blocks on both sides of the streets. There was tension and worry that the violence would erupt again.

The following Saturday, we organized the Uptown Prayer Walk. The police shut down the street for us. We started in our church parking lot with worship, and then we marched from our church down to the mall two blocks away where the big confrontation had been with police and protesters. We set up a stage in that very spot where the SWAT team held the line to protect the mall for hours. We had pastors pray for healing, justice, and peace in our community. It was powerful as hundreds came to walk in the pouring rain. We had government leaders, residents, community activists, police officers, rappers, business owners, pastors, and celebrities. Even hometown hero coach Tony Dungy came to walk with us. It was a powerful day as we worshiped and prayed together. Every news station in our market showed up to cover it. Our tainted frames became a little clearer that day.

WATCH THE HIGHLIGHT VIDEO OF THE UPTOWN PRAYER WALK

Not every community had a healthy multi-ethnic church to lead the way toward peace and reconciliation. The continual stream of racial injustice and political rhetoric from the white evangelical church pushed many people away from God. It literally fogged up their faith frames. In addition, most churches were still physically closed during this time, so people couldn't even grieve in community and get in-person support. It caused many to move further away from their faith and disconnect. Others began to deconstruct their faith and drift into false religions, philosophies, and urban cults that were trending. Some of my personal friends that followed Jesus for decades walked away from their faith. The internet is full of other faith alternatives, and people with tainted frames jumped in headfirst.

MICROFIBER CLOTH FOR YOUR SOUL

It's been frustrating to watch this exodus from the church because Jesus and Justice go together. Justice is a gospel issue. In Matthew 22:39 Jesus told us to love our neighbor as we love ourselves. In Isaiah 1:17, it says, "Learn to do good. Seek justice. Help the oppressed. Defend the cause of the orphans. Fight for the rights of widows." Unfortunately, the word justice has become politicized. This has tainted people's frames from the true biblical mandate we have to treat others in a just way. I understand there have been some Christian-based social justice movements that emphasize good works and exclude the gospel, but justice is not meant to be a replacement for the gospel . . . it should be a result of the gospel. Oxford Languages definition of justice is "just behavior or treatment." If we have a relationship with Jesus, we should be all about that. Matthew 12:18 quotes a prophecy about the Messiah as it says, "Look at my servant, whom I have chosen. He is my beloved, who pleases me. I will put my spirit upon him, and he will proclaim justice to the nations." What if the church would have led the recent fight against racial injustice and oppression? What if the church would have started and led Black Lives Matter? Imagine how different the outcome could have been. Wipe your frames because Jesus and justice go together!

WIPE YOUR
FRAMES
BECAUSE
JESUS AND
JUSTICE GO
TOGETHER

Microfiber cloth is the only eyeglass cleaning cloth accepted by lens manufactures. It is a wipe used for mechanical cleaning to remove dust, dirt, water, or whatever is disturbing the visibility through the lens. The Scriptures are like a microfiber cloth for our souls. At times, we all get some dust, dirt, and grime on our frames. Things we read, watch, listen to, and experience can taint our vision. They can fog up our frames. If we aren't intentional to keep our frames clean, we can begin to live with the layer of haze and see everything differently, but the scary part is what we see through foggy frames isn't always true. A popular term is, "I have to live my truth." My question is, "Is your truth true?" There is a big difference between opinion and truth. "Facts!" Facts is a slang that people say when they hear something they agree with. Many times, people can say "Facts!" when it's not actually solid facts at all. It's just an opinion from someone with tainted frames. The other scary thing is that you can always find someone to confirm your tainted frames' opinion online; some article, some research, some group. Be careful what you expose yourself to and make sure you are regularly using the microfiber cloth of the Scripture to clean your vision.

First John 4 gives us some great advice on how to filter our frames to know what's fact or opinion:

> *Dear friends, do not believe everyone who claims to speak by the Spirit. You must test them to see if the spirit they have comes from God. For there are many false prophets in the world. This is how we know if they have the Spirit of God: If a person claiming to be a prophet acknowledges that Jesus Christ came in a real body, that person has the spirit of God. But if someone claims to be a prophet and does not acknowledge the truth about Jesus, that person is not from God. Such a person has the spirit of the Antichrist, which you heard is coming into the world and indeed is already here. But you belong to God, my dear children, you have already won a victory over those people, because the Spirit who lives in your is greater than the spirit who lives in the world.*

YOU ARE A GATEKEEPER

We live in a world full of tainted frames, but let me encourage you that it is totally possible to stay focused and keep your frames clean. Guard your eye and ear gates and monitor what you allow through them. You've probably heard the term "gatekeepers" before. There are gatekeepers in most industries, politics, government, and so on. I've seen those gatekeepers firsthand in the music industry. They control a large portion of what gets played on radio, playlists, and music placements, but when it comes to your eye and ear gates, you are the gatekeeper. Yes, I know some things we can't help but see or hear when we are out in public, but overall, we still have the majority of control to what we are looking at and listening to. Before we end this chapter, I want you to take some inventory. Let me ask you a couple of questions. What music, conversations, and audio content are you listening to? Those things can protect and develop "clean frames," or they can pollute and dilute your vision.

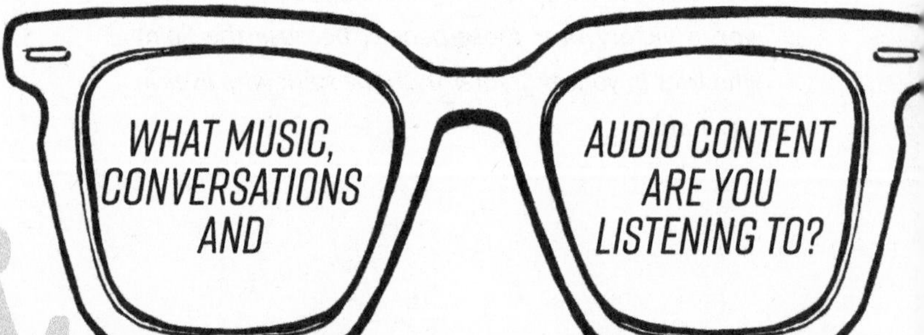

In the gospel of Mark chapter 4, Jesus is teaching and shares about using your light. He says something powerful about our ear gates. Look at verse 23 and 24:

> *If anyone has ears to hear, let him listen. And he said to them, "Pay attention to what you hear. By the measure you use, it will be measured to you—and more will be added to you. For whoever has, more will be given to him, and whoever does not have, even what he has will be taken away from him."*

Jesus said,"Pay attention to what you hear!" Are you paying attention to the music you are listening to, conversations you put yourself in, and audio content you consume? Jesus is really saying, "What you sow into your soul, you will reap more of." The old saying is garbage in garbage what? You already know! I love the way the Message Bible breaks down these two verses: "Are you listening to this? Really listening? Listen carefully to what I am saying and be wary of the shrewd advice that tells you how to get ahead on your own. Giving, not getting, is the way. Generosity begets generosity. Stinginess impoverishes." Our culture is full of shrewd advice on how to get ahead and how to live with tainted frames. Many of us are digesting a regular diet of that daily, and then we wonder why we are struggling with our purity. We wonder why we struggle with negative thoughts. We wonder why we struggle with profanity, lust, discontentment, and anxiety. Take inventory of what you are letting in your ear gates. This isn't 1995 where you are stuck with whatever is on the radio, tape, or CD you have in the car. We have choices, family! We have a computer in our pockets. There are tons of choices… Choose wisely.

The church I lead is known for several things: its innovation, creativity, outreach, diversity… and a big one we're known for is our music. We are big on music. Music speaks to people. It's a language. We have a church full of talented artists, singers, rappers, poets, producers, DJs, filmmakers, and musicians. I grew up playing drums, the trumpet, and Latin percussion. I started rapping when I was thirteen. I've written hundreds of songs, including nine full albums, five Eps, and dozens of features. As an artist, when you are in the studio, you are trying to create music that will connect with people and express a message. Hip-hop and R&B is now the number one consumed music in the US; statista.com reported it was over 31 percent of music listened to in 2020. The second-place category of rock was less than half of that at 15 percent. It's interesting that rock used to be number one, and some of it was known to include blatantly satanic content. Now that hip-hop has shifted into that number-one spot, there seems to be more of this satanic vibe in some of it lately. Lil Nas X had a music video where he gave Satan a lap dance and came out with the controversial Satan shoes. Travis Scott was all over the news for the Astro World Tragedy in Houston, where several people were crushed to death. People described the event like being in hell. There are a lot of people that would call themselves Christians that regularly open their ear gates to this kind of music.

It's interesting at the same time that narrative is going on in hip-hop you've got arguably the biggest artist who had a conversion to Christianity and is producing blatantly Christian music. Kanye West dropped his Jesus Is King album in 2020 that went number one. His Donda was, by far, the biggest-selling album of 2021 up until that point of its release. It sold even more than his previous Jesus Is King project. It was surprising after all that Kanye had been through: he failed in running for president, had mental issues, and got divorced; you didn't hear anything from him for like six months. Then suddenly, he pops back up with these listening parties and packs out stadiums in the middle of a pandemic. Kanye is an anomaly, but I believe many people are attracted to his new content because so many are really hungry right now, and they are spiritually searching. I'm praying for Ye as he is still newer in his walk with God and working through things. It's not perfect; it's messy at times. So was mine the first few years, but I didn't have the pressure of having hundreds of millions of people watching my every move. Pray for him and have grace. The good news is that many people are tired of the same old, tainted hip-hop, and they are looking for something uplifting, positive, and clean.

Is your music pushing you toward clean frames or pulling you away from it? Some of you might say, "I'm not sure where to find good Christian music?" There is lots of incredible Christian hip-hop, R&B, worship, reggae, Spanish music, EDM... whatever you're in the mood for. Search Spotify, Apple Music and YouTube. We can choose to fill our ears with positive uplifting music, podcasts, and audio content. We can choose to walk away from conversations or even shut them down in love when people are gossiping or judging.

My last question is what movies, shows, videos, news, and social media are you looking at? The news can mess you up. It can taint your frames. Psalm 101 is a psalm written by King David. Did you know the Psalms are songs? You gotta check out these lyrics that KD (King David) drops in verse 3, "I will not set before my eyes anything that is worthless. I hate the work of those who fall away; it shall not cling to me." How many of us are rolling like that? If we're honest, we all have some work to do. We regularly allow worthless things to come through our eye gates. Look at that second bar that KD drops: "I hate the work of those that fall away. I won't allow it to cling to me." There are so many Christians that love the tainted frames work of Hollywood, Netflix, HBO, TikTok, and porn websites. Some say, "Wow, this art is just so good," and it clings to them! Some of you might say to me, "But, Pastor T . . . it's not a big deal. It's not going to hurt me. I'm mature. I can handle it."

I'm not saying everything that is secular is bad. I'm not going to that extreme. There can be beauty in music and art even when it isn't directly glorifying God. I'm talking about stuff that is blatantly sinful where it's full of profanity, nudity, adultery, and lying. The stuff that is constantly promoting that lifestyle will taint your frames. When you regularly feed yourself a diet of that kind of stuff through your eye gates, it will cling to you. It will impact you. It will influence you. You will begin to think it's not that big of a deal. Is what you set before your eyes pulling you closer to clean frames or pulling you away? How can you change what you view? How can you keep your frames clean? Two words: intentionality and discipline. You have to be intentional and put up some boundaries of what you are going to look at. Then you have to be disciplined. Boundaries are nothing if you keep crossing them. Many of us need to limit our screen time on our devices. The longer we look, the more undisciplined some of us become, and we can end up putting more and more worthless stuff before our eyes that taints our frames. I'm praying for you to better protect your eye and ear gates to develop cleaner frames.

REFRAME IT

1. Have your frames ever got tainted over a period of time, and you didn't even notice?
2. Did you create any bad habits during the pandemic?
3. What are some ways you can make sure your spiritual frames stay clean?

Watch the Frames Masterclass - Part 3
Log in at *www.tranzlationleadership.com*
and the course will be in your library if you followed the directions at the end of chapter 1.

HUMAN FRAMES VS GOD FRAMES

I'M ONLY HUMAN AFTER ALL . . .

I'm only human. I'm an eighties baby, so I remember the song "Human" by the Human League. Another major eighties hit was "Human Nature" by Michael Jackson. Both of those songs were radio hits that were in the top ten on the charts. A more recent human jam was released in 2016: "Human" by Rag'n'Bone Man. The lyrics of his song say, "Maybe I'm foolish, maybe I'm blind. Thinking I can see through this and see what's behind. Got no way to prove it so maybe I'm blind. But I'm only human after all, I'm only human after all. Don't put your blame on me." With over one billion views on YouTube, it has a message that resonates with so many humans. We're born with human frames, so we can't help but see some things through them. We live in this human body and have a human nature that can pull us in the wrong direction. If we don't keep it in check, it can cause us to think the wrong thoughts, develop selfish motives, and make bad decisions.

Our human frames can influence our judgment. We can look at people and circumstances in a way that is opposite of how our Creator sees them.

Our human frames can cause us to judge people on the outside instead of looking at their heart like God does. Let's be honest that we all do this to some degree. When we first see someone, we can make assumptions by the way they look. It could be their age, gender, clothes, skin color, accent, or a number of other variables we notice. We immediately try to figure out who this person is through our human frames. Many of our assumptions can be completely off. If we get to know the person, we can see how wrong our initial human frame view was.

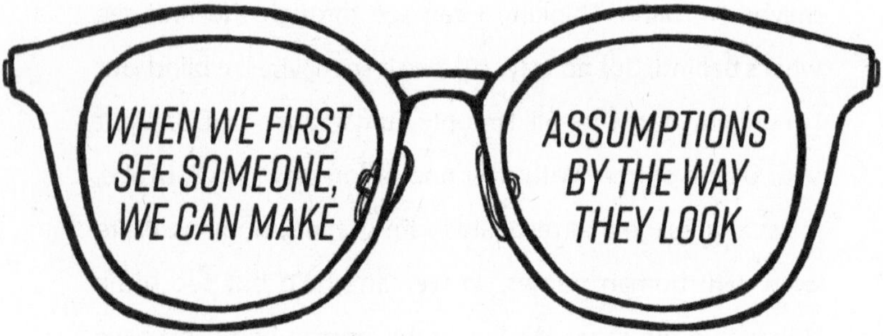

A few years ago, I was standing in the lobby of our church before a special Salsa event. Yes, we get down like that at mi iglesia (my church). I was talking to a lady from our congregation as I was facing the door. I always try to be observant to connect with as many people as I can when I'm in our church lobby. I noticed a guy come in the front door, and he started talking to a new member of our security team. The new security team member made a rookie move and pointed directly to me, and the guy made a beeline straight to me. I knew he asked where the pastor was, and I was right about that part. As I was talking to this lady, I watched him approach and stand behind her, waiting to talk to me next. I admit I was sizing him up with human frames. There had been several guys that week that had stopped by the church looking for money. He looked like them. He didn't look homeless, but he looked like one of those guys that had a story about his car being broken down around the corner, and he needed gas money. Or he needed a bus ticket to go back to Tennessee to be with his family. Or he needed money for a bus pass to go to the hospital to see his sick mother. Trust me, I've heard a million different stories in urban ministry. Usually when you offer a ride, take them to the gas station, or offer to buy them food, they decline… because it's just a story to get cash. At the moment, I was a little jaded and looking at him through human eyes.

The conversation with the lady ended, and I gave her a hug, and then he stepped up, and I was like, "Here we go." Boy, was I wrong! This guy told me that he was with the fireworks company that was going to set up a tent in our parking lot. We had just started a relationship with this company, where they were going to give us 10 percent of their sales if they could use our space. He stopped by to ask me if we could move a vehicle that was in the front area where they were about to set up. Then he went on and on about how impressed he was about all the outreach stuff our church does in the community. I asked him how long he had worked for the fireworks company, and then my jaw dropped. He was the owner with one-hundred-plus locations. I was talking to the main guy that runs this large company. Then he started telling me that he wanted to partner and help us raise money for all the community outreach that we do. I got his number and connected him to our Love Our City team. He and his wife invited us to dinner, and we got to know them better and hear their hearts. The past five years, we've had an incredible partnership that has helped us raise over six figures to go toward our outreach efforts with Love Our City. Even greater than that, we have become friends and have ministered to their family. Just imagine if I would have let my human frames take over and told him that I couldn't talk with him. I would have missed it. Our human frames can cause us to miss incredible opportunities and never get to start amazing relationships.

GOD FRAMES TAKE FAITH

Taking off our human frames takes faith. There are a couple of definitions for faith. In this case, I'm talking about believing in something you can't see. We struggle with this because we are visual people. We want to see it. We want proof. We want it now. In John 14, Jesus told his disciples he was preparing a place for them in heaven and that he would come back and get them when things were ready. In verse 4, Jesus said, *"'And you know the way to where I am going.' Thomas replied, 'No, we don't know, Lord, we have no idea where you are going, so how can we know the way.'"* There was my boy doubting Thomas (that's actually my government name) doing what he did. At the time, he just couldn't see it. He had the wrong frames on, so in faith, he couldn't follow where Jesus was going. What Jesus said next really draws the line in the sand. It separates Christianity from other religions. Our pluralistic human frames society doesn't like this next verse. They want to ignore this part and delete it. They'd like to cancel Jesus for this statement. Jesus told Thomas, "I am the way, the truth and the life. No one can come to the Father except through me. If you had really known me, you would know who my Father is. From now on, you do know him and have seen him!" Wow . . . did you catch that? Jesus said nobody can come to the Father except through him. You can't get to God through Buddha, Muhammed, mediation, crystals, or any other way... only through Jesus. That takes some faith.

In verse 8, Philip responds with human frames and said, *"Lord, show us the Father, and we will be satisfied."* Philip wanted more proof. He wanted to see some type of miracle through his human frames. He still couldn't fully believe. I think Jesus was a little frustrated at this point and said, "Have I been with you all this time, Philip, and yet you still don't know who I am? Anyone who has seen me has seen the Father! So why are you asking me to show him to you?" In verse 11, he told him he'd already seen proof. "Just believe that I am in the Father and the Father is in me. Or at least believe because of the work you have seen me do." I get frustrated with the disciples thinking that I would never doubt if I was in their shoes. They got to roll with Jesus for three years, hear his teaching, and see the miracles firsthand, but many times when you are in the middle of something great, you can look through human frames and take it for granted. You can reason it away or even miss the miracle. The Holy Spirit has checked me multiple times and reminded me of all of the miracles that I have seen and been part of. Even with all of the amazing things I've seen, it's easy to slip on the human frames and doubt that we can overcome the next obstacle in front of us. Looking through the wrong frames can make the giants look much bigger than they actually are.

4

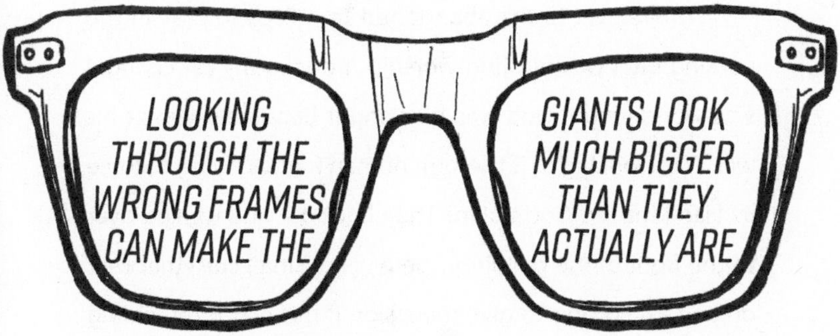

LOOKING THROUGH THE WRONG FRAMES CAN MAKE THE
GIANTS LOOK MUCH BIGGER THAN THEY ACTUALLY ARE

At the end of 2009, our church was in a limbo period. It was very challenging looking at it through human frames. The giants looked huge. We were trying to finalize the sale our church building as it had been under contract for close to a year. We had to extend the closing date multiple times as the church buying it couldn't get their financing lined up. We were in the middle of a recession, and banks weren't excited about loaning money to churches. On the other hand, we were negotiating with Toys R' Us to take over one of their closed locations. We had been engaged with these wonderful toy people for close to eighteen months. Both situations were dragging. I was discouraged. I was doubting. I was tired. When you feel like that, the human frames can start to slide back on. Looking through those frames, it seemed like an impossible situation. When you rock the human frames, the human thoughts become the soundtrack; "What were we thinking? We bit off more than we could chew. This is going to be a huge failure. Everything is about to fall apart."

I drove over to the abandoned Toys R' Us to pray in the parking lot. I was blasting worship music in my car crying. I was wondering if God was blocking it because it wasn't his will. Was I looking at it through human frames trying to force it? Had I missed God's plan? Then I got out and walked over to the front of the building. There was a small curb that I sat on and asked God to give me a sign if this was the building for our church. God has a sense of humor. He can sometimes invade our frames with an answer from very unconventional sources. I looked up behind me, and the windows were boarded up with posters plastered across them. The vibrant posters were for the Michael Jackson documentary, This Is It! I busted out laughing. You can't make these things up. Michael Jackson is in this pose that actually looks like he is worshiping (Google it and see!).

THE BLESSER IS GREATER THAN THE BLESSING

In Luke 5, it records that Jesus was teaching by the shore of the sea of Galilee, and the crowd was pushing closer and closer, so Jesus jumped in a fishing boat and asked the owner to push out a little bit from the shoreline. Jesus taught the crowd from the boat. When he finished his sermon, he looked over at the boat owner and told him to go out into deeper water and cast his fishing nets. The boat owner was looking at the situation through human frames. At first, he argued because they hadn't caught any fish all night. He was tired. They were cleaning their nets and getting ready to go home. Sometimes God gives us instructions, and we argue that it will never work. When we look through our human frames, we can be blinded to the possibilities. After doubting and complaining, this boat owner agreed to follow Jesus's request. The Scripture tells us they caught so many fish that their nets started to tear. Now, this wasn't flimsy fishing gear; they had professional nets. It was the biggest catch they had ever seen in their lives. The catch was so big they called another boat over to help. There were so many fish that both boats started to sink. This boat owner's human frames were smashed, and he was experiencing a miracle. His name was Simon Peter. He fell at Jesus's feet. Jesus told him and his crew that from now on, they wouldn't be catching fish, but they would be catching people. They brought their boats back to land, left everything, and followed Jesus! Wait, what? They just had the best fishing day ever, and they quit? Their human frames were exchanged for a pair of God frames. They now had new vision and purpose for their lives.

PETER AND HIS SQUAD WOULD RATHER BE
WITH THE BLESSER THAN WITH THE BLESSING

Peter and his squad would rather be with the blesser than with the blessing. On the contrary, people with human frames end up worshiping the creation instead of the Creator, but when you reframe it, you see that the one who made everything is so much better than the stuff he made. Let's be honest, it can be tough to fight back our human frames. We like the created. We like the stuff. We like buying things. If you asked people to choose between a million dollars and a relationship with God… many would choose the money. The richest man that ever lived was asked by God what he wanted. He could have asked for riches and pleasure, but instead, he just asked for wisdom. As a result of the wisdom that God blessed him with, his wealth and influence exponentially increased. His name was King Solomon. I've watched money and possessions change people for the worse or the better. It depends on what frames they were rocking. Even King Solomon slid the human frames back on as life went on. He got blinded by some of his wives and started to entertain worship of other gods. In the end, he realized his mistakes and admitted that riches are meaningless without God. The creation doesn't compare to the Creator.

In the gospel of Mark chapter 8, Jesus healed a blind man at Bethsaida. Then he and his team left and headed to the villages near Caesarea Philippi. As they were walking along, Jesus asked his crew, "Who do people say I am?" They replied, "Some say John the Baptist, some say Elijah, and others say you are one of the other prophets." Then Jesus asked them, "But who do you say I am?" Peter, the fisherman, jumped in and dropped a truth bomb. He replied, "You are the Messiah!" Peter got a revelation that Jesus was the Messiah they had been waiting for. Jesus didn't deny this but warned his team to keep that to themselves. Then he predicted his death. Verse 31 says, "Then Jesus began to tell them the Son of Man must suffer many terrible things and be rejected by the elders, the leading priests, and the teachers of religious law. He would be killed, but three days later he would rise from the dead." Peter pulled Jesus aside and rebuked him for saying he was going to die. He thought he was helping. In today's language, it might have sounded like, "Jesus, come here, bro. My guy, what are you talking about? You're sounding a little crazy right now. Listen, you are not going to be killed by anyone. I'm your ride or die. I got your back. Nobody is going to lay a hand on you. So please stop talking this dying nonsense stuff to the squad. You are scaring everyone and bringing down the vibe. You just fed 4,000 people and healed a blind guy. This ministry tour is fire, and everyone loves you. Your Instagram account is blowing up. You might have some haters, but don't worry about it. It's all good. You are the Messiah, and nobody can touch you."

What was Jesus's response to Peter? "Jesus turned around and looked at his disciples, then reprimanded Peter. 'Get away from me, Satan!' he said. 'You are seeing things merely from a human point of view, not from God's.'" Ok, so Peter just had this revelation that Jesus was the Messiah, then he pulls him aside thinking he is protecting him and being loyal, and Jesus calls him Satan? Wow. Really? That seems harsh at first glance. Did you catch the second part that Jesus said? This explains it. He basically said, "Peter, you are seeing things through human frames and not through God frames." It was the Messiah's purpose to come and die for the sins of his people. Peter couldn't see that through his human frames and didn't want to hear any talk about dying. He loved Jesus and wanted to continue to be with him. He thought he was encouraging Jesus and giving him a pep talk. Peter had a revelation and then a rebuke. The revelation for Peter was that Jesus was the Messiah; the rebuke was for trying to stop the Messiah's mission. In context, Jesus wasn't actually calling him Satan. He was calling out Satan who was influencing Peter's thinking at that moment. Satan was causing Peter to see the situation through human frames.

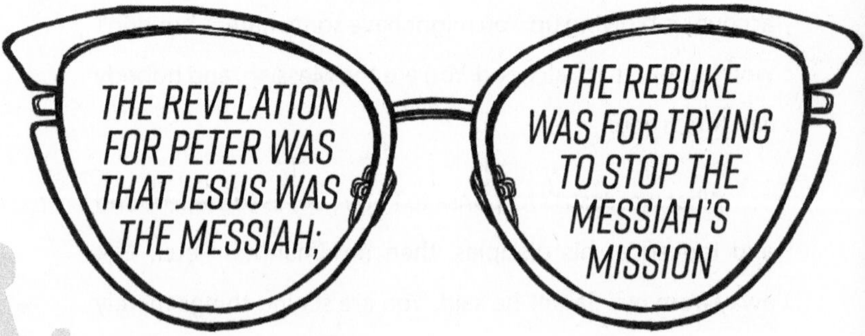
THE REVELATION FOR PETER WAS THAT JESUS WAS THE MESSIAH;
THE REBUKE WAS FOR TRYING TO STOP THE MESSIAH'S MISSION

There are so many times when we see things just like Peter. We are looking through a human point of view and not from God's. I don't believe that Christians can be possessed by Satan or demons, but we can be influenced by them. In balance, this doesn't mean that every time we have a bad thought or do something bad that the devil made us do it. Some Christians try to blame everything bad on Satan. Stop that! He's not that powerful. Many times, you are simply putting on human frames and are tempted by your own flesh. The book of James reminds us that "Temptation comes from our own desires, which entice us and drag us away." We have to keep our human nature in check and also guard against Satan trying to influence us in any way.

Here is the last thing I'll say about human frames. I love this part. Second Corinthians 5 tells us that we are God's street team! I was part of a street team before where we would go and give out flyers, stickers, mix CDs, and even illegally hang up posters all over the city. In this passage of Scripture, my guy Paul tells us that we are God's ambassadors. He shares that we have died to our old life. We're new people. Look at what he drops in verse 16, "So we have stopped evaluating others from a human point of view. At one time we thought of Christ merely from a human point of view. How differently we know him now! This means that anyone who belongs to Christ has become a new person. The old life is gone; a new life has begun!" Now that we are a new people, we have to stop looking at others through human frames. We have to learn to see them through God's frames. When we do that, we no longer see their problems. We see their potential. God can give us supernatural strength to push past their issues and lean into their purpose.

Paul also reminds us that at one point, we looked at Christ through human frames. Maybe we were skeptical or just uninterested, but now we know him. We are brand new. Now we can clearly see our mission that is laid out in verse 19: "For God was in Christ, reconciling the world to himself, no longer counting people's sins against them. And he gave us this wonderful message of reconciliation. So we are Christ's ambassadors; God is making his appeal through us. We speak for Christ when we plead, 'Come back to God!'" We should feel some weight from that part that says God is making his appeal through us. Nobody else is coming. It's us. So how does your appeal look? Is it appealing? Let's be brutally honest . . . most Christians' appeal needs work. Mine could be better, so I'm guessing yours could use an upgrade as well. That's why we're on this frames journey together. The world has their own set of frames on as they look at us. We have to show them something different that stands out. It won't always look appealing in a cool way. That's okay. It has to be authentic and consistent. We are God's street team. Many people in the world are tired of looking through fuzzy frames. They long for something more. We have it.

REFRAME IT:

1. Have you ever looked at someone through human frames and got it all wrong?
2. Have you ever doubted God's instructions because you were looking through human frames? What happened?
3. If you have a relationship with Jesus, you are now on his street team. In what ways can you better represent him and get the word out?

Watch the Frames Masterclass - Part 4
Log in at *www.tranzlationleadership.com*
and the course will be in your library if you followed the directions at the end of chapter 1.

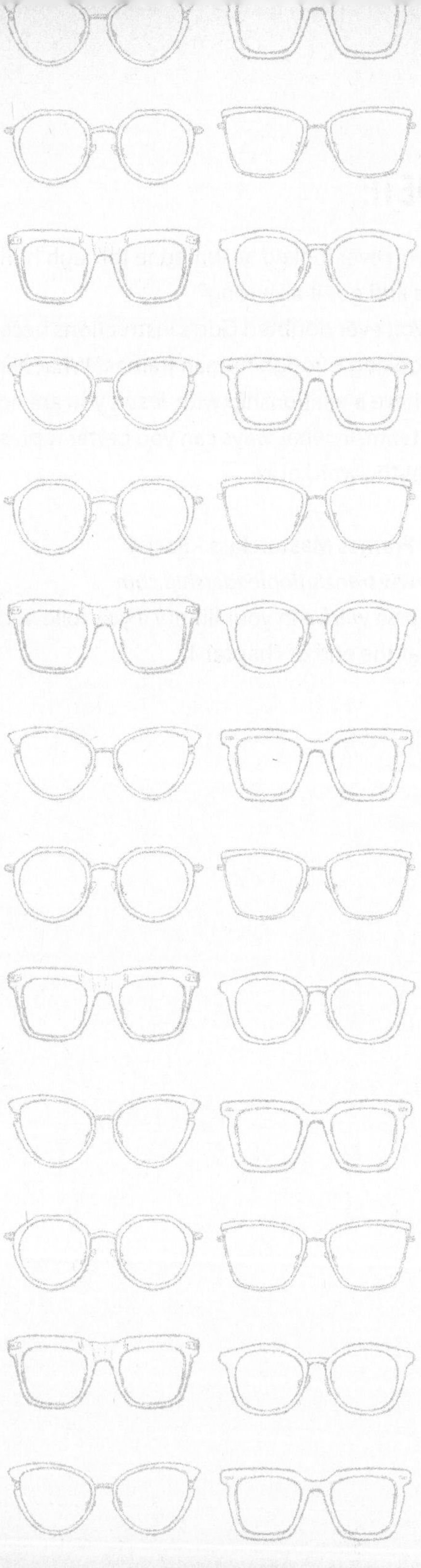

5

GREEDY FRAMES VS GENEROUS FRAMES

GOD DON'T PLAY

Some of the scariest stories in the Bible to me are ones about greed. In Acts 5, there was this couple that sold a piece of property and made a public display that they were giving all of the proceeds to the church. They didn't have to do this, but they said they were going to. It sounds like this couple wanted their fifteen minutes of fame on the gram. They presented a big check to the disciples at Sunday Service, telling everyone how they were giving the entire amount to the Lord's work. This couple was rocking greedy frames. Look at what really happened: "But there was a certain man named Ananias who, with his wife, Sapphira, sold some property. He brought part of the money to the apostles claiming it was the full amount. With his wife's consent, he kept the rest." So, they wanted to shine in front of everyone, but their greed caused them to lie and hold back some of the money on the side. Here is the scary part in verse 3:

Then Peter said, "Ananias, why have you let Satan fill your heart? You lied to the Holy Spirit, and you kept some of the money yourself. The property was yours to sell or not to sell as you wished. And after selling it, the money was also yours to give away. How could you do a thing like this? You weren't lying to us but to God!" As soon as Ananias heard these words, he fell to the floor and died. Everyone who heard about it was terrified. Then some young men got up, wrapped him in a sheet, and took him out and buried him.

GOD DON'T PLAY

They didn't have cell phones or social media back then. You know this would have gone viral on every platform, and people would have been texting Sapphira, telling her, "Girl, your husband dropped dead for lying to God. You need to get up here to the church ASAP FrFr!" But his wife had no idea because look what happened next: "About three hours later his wife came in, not knowing what had happened. Peter asked her, 'Was this the price you and your husband received for your land?' 'Yes,' she replied, 'that was the price.'" Peter replied with a gangster-type authority in verse 9:

And Peter said, "How could the two of you even think of conspiring to test the Spirit of the Lord like this? The young men who buried your husband are at the door, and they will carry you out too." Instantly, she fell to the floor and died. When the young men came in and saw that she was dead, they carried her out and buried her beside her husband. Great fear gripped the entire church and everyone else who heard what had happened.

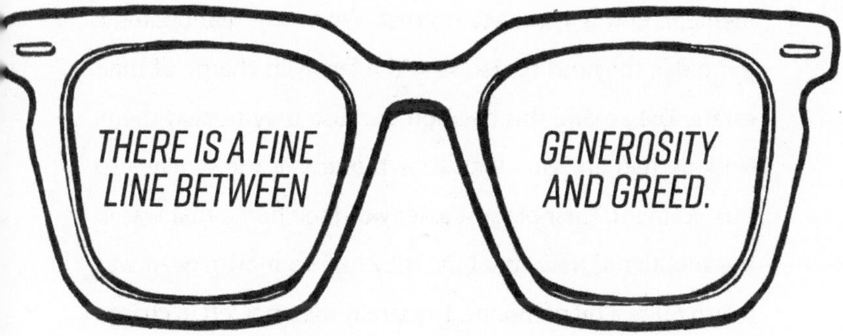
THERE IS A FINE LINE BETWEEN
GENEROSITY AND GREED.

The crazy thing about this story is that it includes generosity. Lots of people sell their property, stocks, or cryptocurrency and don't give any of it to a local church, charity, or non-profit organization. Ananias and Sapphire could have kept all of it, or at least just tithed off of it. There is a fine line between generosity and greed. They lied. Their greed canceled out their generosity. Some people are generous for the wrong reasons. I know that some of you are thinking, "Must be nice to have a property to sell. I'm not ballin' like that," but hold up; greed is a temptation for all economic contexts. Greed doesn't depend on how much people have but on how much of what they have has them. Go back and read that last sentence again. Greed and corruption can be found in both the materially rich and materially poor. Some of the most corrupt leaders in the world are in the poorest countries.

Greedy frames can turn a trusted friend or family member into a lying scam artist. When my grandparents got older, they put someone in the family in charge of their estate. They made this decision because they trusted them. Nobody had an issue with it as the rest of the family also trusted them. Their biggest asset was their home that was in the suburbs of New York City. They had no mortgage. It was worth quite a bit of money. The family member left in charge sold it and promised to send checks equally to everyone as the will required. My mother got a small portion of the money (not her full share), but none of the other siblings received anything. The person in charge literally disappeared. She moved, changed numbers, and didn't want to be found. Her greedy frames cut off all family ties for the rest of her life. We later found out that the majority of the money was spent at the casinos in Atlantic City. It was all gone. She even lost her own home. It was devastating to the rest of the family. What my grandparents worked their whole lives for was stolen and gambled away. This kind of stuff happens every day when people slide on the frames of greed.

Another scary greed story is found in the Old Testament book of Joshua. This is where the Israelites were entering and taking over the promised land. It starts with the miracle story of marching around the city of Jericho, watching the walls fall down, and the Israelites taking the city. Wow, imagine watching that miracle take place right before your eyes. Be careful because greed can pop up right in the middle of a miracle! God told them to destroy the city but take all of the gold, silver, and valuables and bring it into God's treasury. He warned them if they took anything for themselves, they would bring trouble on themselves and the entire camp of Israel. When you have greedy frames on, you don't take heed to caution. You don't read the warning labels. You don't think about the possible consequences. You get blinded by your own selfish gain. A solider named Achan was fighting while wearing greedy frames, and when he was recovering the plunder he couldn't help himself. He found a Louie Vuitton robe from Babylon, 200 silver coins, and a bar of gold. Achan took them and hid them under his tent. He was able to hide his greed from everyone around him, but God saw it. You and I might be able to disguise our greedy frames from others, but our Creator knows our hearts and sees what we do in secret.

BE CAREFUL
BECAUSE GREED
CAN POP UP
RIGHT IN THE
MIDDLE OF A
MIRACLE.

God warned that if anyone disobeyed his instructions about Jericho that they would bring trouble on themselves and everyone. The Israelites had just been part of this amazing miracle taking down the walls of Jericho, so they were confident to take over the next city in the promised land. They sent spies out to the town of Ai and decided that they didn't even need to send the whole army. This would be an easy win for the team. Boy were they wrong. The men of Ai defeated them, chased them, and killed dozens of men. The Bible says in Joshua 7:5, "The Israelites were paralyzed with fear at this turn of events, and their courage melted away." Joshua and the leaders of Israel cried out to God, wondering why he would lead them into the promised land to be defeated. Look at what God said to them in chapter 7 verse 10-12:

> *Get up! Why are you lying on your face like this? Israel has sinned and broken my covenant! They have stolen some of the things that I have commanded must be set*

apart for me. And they have not only stolen them but have lied about it and hidden the things among their belongings. That is why the Israelites are running from their enemies in defeat. For not Israel itself has been set apart for destruction. I will not remain with you any longer unless you destroy the things among you that were set apart for destruction.

Joshua had each tribe present themselves before the leaders, and the Lord pointed out the tribe of Judah. Eventually, that led to Achan being singled out. He confessed what he took. The soldiers went under his tent and removed the items. In verse 25, Joshua said to Achan, "Why have you brought trouble on us? The Lord will now bring trouble on you." Achan and his family were stoned to death, and they burned their bodies. This one man's greed affected the entire country. It cost dozens of men their lives and took out his whole family. Greedy frames can make you feel the selfish moves are worth it, but in the end, it doesn't add up. You always lose.

YOU ARE RICH!

Yes, I'm talking to you. You are absolutely, positively, incredibly rich. Now, you might be thinking I'm talking about being spiritually rich because we are God's children. Nope! I'm talking about real-deal rich. Yup, that's you. Yup, that's me.

That's us! Most Americans don't feel rich, and we are. Most of you reading this don't feel rich because there are others out there that are a lot richer than us, and we compare ourselves to them… so we feel broke, but we are in a bubble, a rich bubble. We have #richpeopleproblems. Most of you have a car, and if you do, that puts you in the top 10 percent of people in the world. Most of you drove your car this week and went to a restaurant to eat or get take-out where somebody took your order, cooked for you, and cleaned up after you. Then many of you drove home, and when you pulled up, you pressed a button, a door magically opened up, and you parked your car in its own room. Cars have their own rooms in our country. We're rich! But many people have so much extra stuff they fill their car's room up, and their car can't even fit in there. We walk into our house, and it's climate-controlled. We have a bathroom in our house—many of us have two or three of them, and we press a button, and our stuff disappears, while many people in the world just have a hole in the ground to do their business. There are several websites online where you can type in your annual income, and it will give you an estimate of where you are compared to the rest of the planet. If you make six figures, you are generally in the top 3 percent. Even if you are at America's poverty level for a family of four, you are still in the top 20 percent.

ON A GLOBAL SCALE, WE'RE VERY RICH
BUT WE'RE NOT VERY GENEROUS.

On a global scale, we're very rich, but we're not very generous. lendingtree.com found that only 56% of Americans donated to charity in 2021 at an average of $574. [1] That means 44% didn't give anything. For many people, the greedy frames get thicker as they gain more wealth. Lots of people have a desire to give more, but they feel like they can't. I grew up with a scarcity mentality. When I was younger, my family was lower-income, and when we went to McDonald's, my sister and I would literally have to split a cheeseburger. So if you grew up in the struggle and haven't learned to trust God, you can have a scarcity mentality. Even if you didn't grow up splitting burgers, you can still develop scarcity frames because the majority of Americans live paycheck to paycheck. God supplies… then we consume, lack, fear, and repeat. It's a cycle of scarcity. If you are getting a little tense right now and your butt cheeks just tightened up, you might have a scarcity mentality. I'm just saying. Just relax and breathe. We are five chapters in now. We're like family. Pull up a chair, and let's talk.

[1] Dawn Papandrea, "56% of Americans Donated to Charity in 2021", www.lendingtree.com, November 29th, 2021.

MINDSET SHIFT

I want to show you the mindset that Christ-followers should have. Because of what God did through Jesus, it creates a whole different cycle, not a cycle of scarcity but a cycle of supply. Paul talked about Generosity and breaks down this cycle of supply in 2 Corinthians 9:7-11:

> *You must decide in your heart how much to give. And don't give reluctantly or in response to pressure. For God loves a person who gives cheerfully. And God will generously provide all you need. Then you will always have everything you need and plenty left over to share with others. As the scriptures say, "They share freely and give generously to the poor. Their good deeds will be remembered forever." For God is the one who provides seed for the farmer and then bread to eat. In the same way, he will provide and increase your resources and then produce a great harvest of generosity in you. Yes, you will be enriched in every way so that you can always be generous. And when we take your gifts to those who need them, they will thank God.*

I get to regularly watch these verses come to life, and I love it! My church does this Love Our City week and several other serving days throughout the year. People are generous and give, then God multiplies it as we go and serve thousands of people in our community. Those people who receive the generosity thank God. We've seen hundreds of them then come to our church, and many start a relationship with Christ, get baptized, and are plugged into the family. It's beautiful to watch this passage play out in real life.

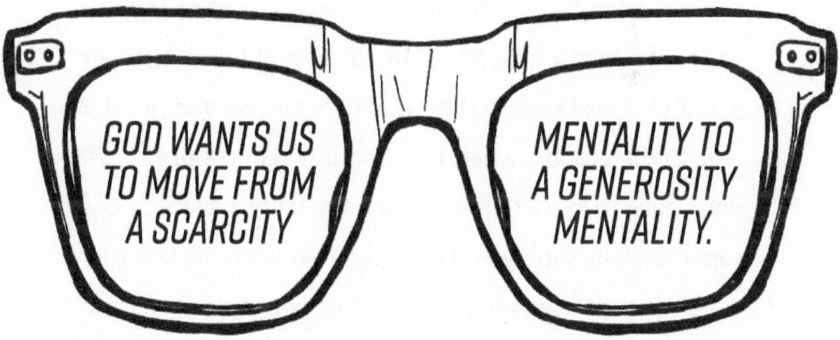
GOD WANTS US TO MOVE FROM A SCARCITY
MENTALITY TO A GENEROSITY MENTALITY.

God wants us to move from a scarcity mentality to a generosity mentality. Developing generous frames is based on the principle that God owns everything. This prescription helps us clearly see that we are managers. Greedy frames tell me the opposite. It prescribes a fake prescription that makes me see everything as mine, but how is it truly mine if I can't take any of it with me when I die? The reality is that we only get to hold it for a minute. I've learned to live and lead with an open hand. God has given me resources to steward for this season. Someday, we'll all have to stand before our Creator and give an account for what we did with what we were given.

How do we switch frames and move into a generosity mentality? Here's how the generosity cycle of supply works. When we get our paycheck that God supplied, the first thing we do is give some of it. This is actually an act of worship. We give back to the one who supplied it. God was generous with us first as he gave his Son Jesus so we could be forgiven and made brand new. We didn't deserve it, we didn't earn it, but God was generous to us. When we give and put that seed in the ground, what does God do? He multiplies it. We don't have to fear like the scarcity mentality. We watch God supernaturally supply and multiply what we have, and then we grow. We've seen it work, and then we repeat the cycle. God supplies, we give, he multiplies, we grow, and we repeat.

Instead of living with the fear of lack, we take this crazy leap of faith and level up and give. It might not always seem to make sense, but we do it and watch God show up. This is what happens when we put on generous frames. We level up, but just saying the word generous can be somewhat vague and general. What does it really mean? How much, and how often? How does the generosity thing really work? It doesn't deal with a certain amount as we are all at different financial levels.

Giving one hundred dollars to someone might be everything he or she has, while to someone else, it might be like giving ten cents. A percentage makes it equal for everyone. Remember, I said the average American only gives 2.8 percent of his or her income. God's desire is that we start with giving 10 percent of our income. In the Bible, it is called a "tithe." It comes from the Hebrew word mahaser, which means a tenth. A tenth of everything God blesses us with we bring back to him as an act of worship. Some people ask or even argue that it doesn't matter as some of these parts of the Bible were written in the Old Testament under the religious law, but if you do your research, you can find that Abraham brought a tithe to the priest before the law was in place. Then you can also go to the New Testament and find where Jesus affirms tithing in Matthew 23:23. He says you should tithe, but don't forget the more important matters. In other words, tithing is some of the basics . . . but don't forget love, mercy, and grace!

Here are two thoughts about tithing. Maybe you've never heard of it, or you don't fully understand why we should do it. You might be suspect of it like I was at one point in my life. The first thought is that the tithe teaches us to put God first. Check out Deuteronomy 14:23, where it says tithing will teach you to always have fear (reverence and respect) for God. Many people will regularly say God is number one in their lives, but if you look at their lives and finances, that is clearly not the case. Tithing teaches you to really put him as number one in your life. I know some of you are thinking… if I was going to start tithing regularly, I would have to rearrange my whole life around God. Boom! That's the point. It does take crazy faith to go from 2 or 3 percent giving to 10 percent. My family has entirely rearranged our lives to put God first in our finances, and I've got stories for days of how God has multiplied and shows up again and again.

The second thought about tithing is that it builds our faith. Malachi 3:10–11 shares, *"'Bring the whole tithe into the storehouse [The local church—God's house], that there may be food in my house. Test me in this,' says the Lord."* This is the only spot in the Bible where God invites people to test him. He's saying, "Try it." Look at what it says the result will be in the next verse: "And see if I will not throw open the floodgates of heaven and pour out so much blessing that there will not be room enough to store it." In context, this does not mean money is going to rain down, but it does mean that God will bless and provide for you when you have generous frames on. Many times, he will do that in ways money can't buy: with health, peace, and contentment. God is basically saying in this passage, "See if my economy is different than the world's." You've already tried consume, lack, fear, repeat… but have you really tried give, multiply, grow, repeat?

NEW MUSCLES

Generosity is like a muscle. I work out three times a week. If I told you to drop down and give me fifty push-ups in a row, the average person couldn't do it. Maybe you could do ten or twenty, but if you started doing daily push-ups, then next week, you could probably do five or six more in a row; in a month, maybe fifteen or twenty more. In six months, you might be able to do fifty or close to it. You have to build your muscles. A few years ago on Father's Day, we did a push-up challenge at our church. I challenged any dad that could beat me would get one hundred dollars. I started training and doing push-ups almost every day. That Father's Day, I dropped down and did eighty-eight push-ups in a row. In the first service, the highest dad did sixty-five. In the second service, there was a CrossFit competitor who did ninety-nine, and in the third service, a guy who recently got out of prison did 101. It was a lot of fun, and it pushed a lot of us to get in better shape. Before the training, I could do around fifty, but I pushed myself and grew those muscles to almost double my strength. As you start giving and being generous, you may feel it and be a little sore at first, but as you grow that generosity muscle and start giving consistently, you get stronger. You'll watch God show up, multiply things, give a little more, and get a little stronger in this area of your life. My wife and I started giving 10 percent of our income, and over time, we try to give a little more each year. I'm not saying that to brag but to encourage you that as you give, God will multiply things and grow your faith and your resources. It begins to change your life, and as you give to your local church, you can see it changing other lives around you. As your generous frames activate, you'll begin to realize it really is more blessed to give than receive.

AS YOUR GENEROUS FRAMES ACTIVATE YOU'LL BEGIN

TO REALIZE IT REALLY IS MORE BLESSED TO GIVE THAN RECEIVE

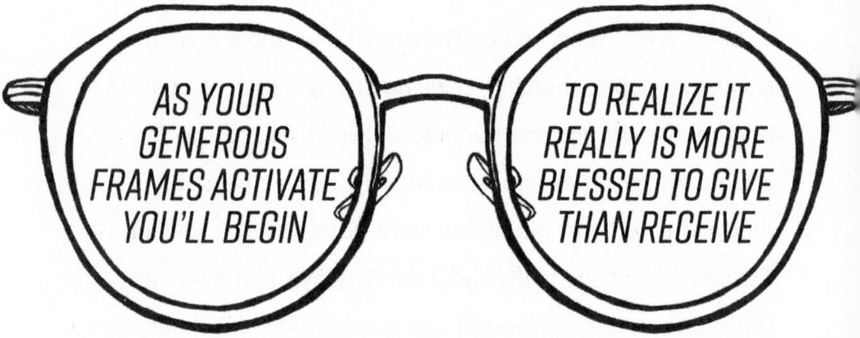

Let me also be honest because I want to set you up to win. It's not always a season of abundance, even when you have generous frames on. There have been seasons in our lives when we were tithing and beyond and things still got tight. Our margins would get depleted, and our savings got low. We still had everything we needed, but it still got really tight. Those are testing moments. We can be tempted to cut back our giving or stop altogether. We stayed consistent. We always watched God come through. We never told anybody, but people would bless us with something we needed. There were four years in a row where we got to take a vacation that was paid for by an organization or individual. We were worn out doing ministry sixty hours a week but didn't have any extra money to go away and rest. God saw what we needed, and he provided. My wife and I were even blessed to go to Hawaii for one week on a marriage retreat at this five-star resort, all expenses paid. It was a trip we'll never forget. We watch God come through again and again when we live and give with generous frames.

REFRAME IT:

1. Have greedy frames ever caused a trusted friend or family member to do something you wouldn't have expected?
2. Do you currently operate in more of a scarcity mentality or generosity mentality?
3. Have you watched God provide and do a miracle when you were consistently giving and being generous?

Watch the Frames Masterclass - Part 5
Log in at *www.tranzlationleadership.com*
and the course will be in your library if you followed the directions at the end of chapter 1.

6

ENTITLED FRAMES VS GRATEFUL FRAMES

GENERATIONAL ISSUES

There was a consultant in Philadelphia that worked with college graduates. He was doing a workshop with them and said that everyone in the work force today uses a word for the generation entering the work force, and it starts with an E. He asked the graduates what they thought the E word was, and so these young hopefuls said, "Energetic, Excellent, Exceptional… " They kept going for a while and, finally, the consultant burst their bubble and said, "Actually the word is ENTITLED." Boom!

Millennials were labeled as the entitled generation, but now Gen Z has taken it up a notch. I saw this article saying Gen Z workers are terrifying their millennial bosses with entitled demands. They delegate work to their bosses. They actually tell the CEO, "No thank you; you need to do that task." They demand the company supports activist causes they think are important. They take PTO for anxiety. They don't call in to take time off; instead, they text their boss that they aren't coming in today because they are not in a good place mentally.

Now before all you Millennials, Gen-xers, and Boomers start jumping on Gen Z, we have to realize we've created this generation by our actions and attitudes. So we're all in this! How did we do that, you ask? Many people that are Gen X and older worked way too much, and there was lots of divorce. People loved their kids, so they tried to make up the lack of time by rarely saying no. "Yes, you can have this and you can have that… "They thought they could just make more money and give them more stuff. So younger generations have been spoiled a lot more. I know my kids have way more stuff than I did at their ages.

On top of all of that, we protected and sheltered the upcoming generation a lot more. When I was the youth pastor in the nineties, we stuffed twenty-seven kids in a fifteen-passenger van. Seatbelts? We didn't even have any as the van was from the seventies. We actually only had three rows of seats as the fourth row was taken out so we could haul things around. That majorly cut down our seating capacity, so I got creative and started the original crate challenge. We put milk crates back there for kids to sit on. Genius! They loved it. Everybody fought to sit in the back on the crates, and guess what? Nobody died. Today, we have multiple seatbelts for kids, and they sit in a car seat backward until they are like nine. We cover them in hand sanitizer. They must wear knee pads when skateboarding. You can't even ride a bike without a helmet. They are totally protected!

Wait, there is more! When I was a kid, you used to actually have to win something to get a trophy. Anyone remember that? Now, you just have to show up. They call it a participation trophy. It's like, "Hey little Billy, you were in last place because you ran so slow. We're so proud of you; here's a trophy, buddy! Congrats for being in last place!" Wait, what? That has helped build a few generations of people that are kind of entitled.

Before you old people reading this start feeling all righteous… you are ratchet too! It's not just them; it's me, it's you, it's us!

We now have a computer in our pockets and have apps on it that can do almost anything. We can order a car to pick us up, order a pizza, or order a kitchen sink on Amazon that will arrive by tomorrow. We love convenience, but if there is a little spinning circle on our screen for more than 2.5 seconds, we start getting upset. We get so upset with slow Wi-Fi! Just a few years ago, there was no Wi-Fi on our phones, but now that we have it, we want everything immediately. All generations are now wearing entitled frames.

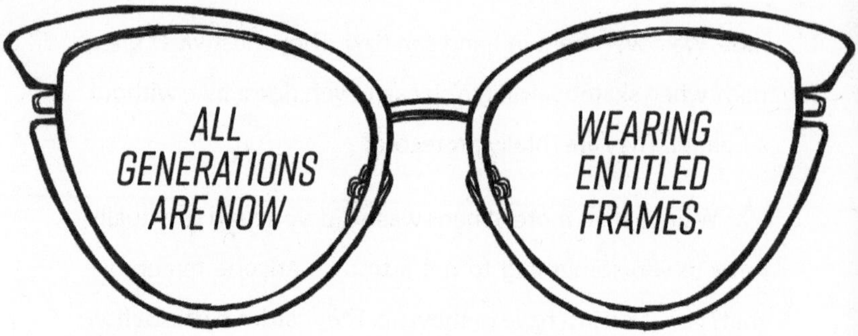
ALL GENERATIONS ARE NOW
WEARING ENTITLED FRAMES.

NO THANK YOU'S

This chapter is going to focus on the opposite of entitlement. We're going to zoom in on gratitude. I'm grateful you made it to this part of the book! This is the good part. There's a very interesting story about some people who looked entitled and almost all of them didn't stop to show any gratitude. In Luke 17, Jesus was on tour with his crew and got noticed. In verse 11, it says, "As Jesus continued on toward Jerusalem, he reached the border between Galilee and Samaria. As he entered a village there, ten lepers stood at a distance, crying out, 'Jesus, Master, have mercy on us!'"

Let's pause for a minute so I can give you some context. Lepers are not common in our culture today. So you probably don't have the full picture. A leper had one of the most painful diseases you could imagine. They had these oozing sores. The sickness would affect their nerve endings, and it was super painful. They could go to sleep in the middle of the night, and because of their sores, they might wake up and find that a rat ate off their pinky. Seriously! There wasn't just the physical pain, but there was also the social pain. They were banned from being around anyone healthy. They were excommunicated! They were in a permanent quarantine. Leviticus 13 says whenever someone got close, they had to scream out "Unclean! Unclean!" By law, they had to warn people to run away. Imagine how humiliating that was. So these people were hurting physically, emotionally, and spiritually. They couldn't go to church or be involved in a small group. They couldn't get prayed for or serve on a ministry team. They were literally cut off from any relationships, contact, or intimacy. Some of them hadn't had a hug in years.

These ten lepers saw this guy rolling up that everyone was talking about. It was rumored that he could heal people. They were freaking out; this could be there chance to be freed of their lockdown restrictions. So they were crying out to Jesus, "Have mercy on us!" When Jesus saw them, look what he said, "Go show yourselves to the priests. And as they went they were cleansed of their leprosy." Did you catch that part… as they went? They weren't actually healed in that moment, but they had to have faith and follow Jesus's instructions. Jesus was testing them. They could have looked down at their hands still all busted up with sores and said, "Why would I go show myself to the priests; nothing has changed." Sometimes God can heal people right away, but other times, he requires some action first. AS THEY WENT, they were healed!

Some of you reading this have been asking God to heal you of your anxiety, addiction, heartbreak, or ___(fill in the blank)___. Maybe Jesus is calling you to do something in faith, and AS YOU GO, your healing will begin to happen. That's a word for someone reading this right now.

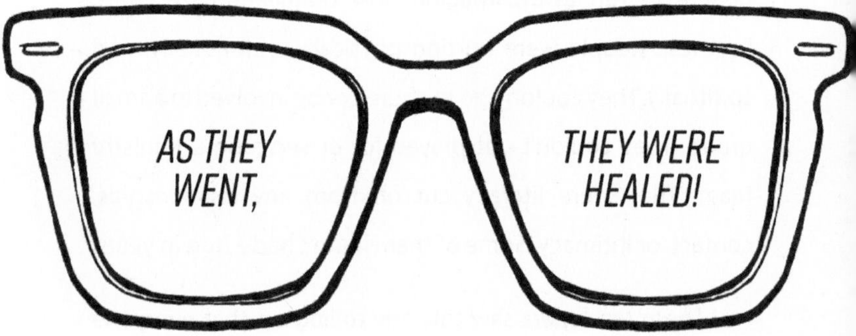
AS THEY WENT,
THEY WERE HEALED!

Can you imagine as these guys were walking to see the priest and they started looking down at their hands, their skin was healing right before their eyes? They were looking at each other like, "Hey bro, your face, it's clearing up! Your ear just grew back! You look normal again! OMG, this is crazy!" By the time they got to the priests, they were probably partying! Look at the shocking part that happens next in verse 15:

One of them, when he saw that he was healed, came back to Jesus shouting, "Praise God." He fell to the ground at Jesus' feet, thanking him for what he has done. This man was a Samaritan. Jesus asked, "Didn't I heal ten men? Where are the other nine? Has no one returned to give glory to God except this foreigner?"

Wait, what? Only one guy came back to say thank you, and he was the Samaritan, the foreigner? In Luke 10, it describes Samaritans as despised. People back then didn't like Samaritans (this was before Jesus remixed their title to Good Samaritans). They were known as the bad guys, but the Samaritan was the only grateful one that came back to say thanks. He was the only one that stopped to thank God for his blessings.

WILL YOU BE THE ONE?

My question to you today is this: Will you be the one? Because truthfully, the odds are stacked against you. Will you be the one that daily pauses to give glory and honor to the one who gave you life? Will you be the one to stop in all the busyness and lift up a true heartfelt worship to the Creator and Sustainer of the universe? Will you be the one to give praise and worship to the one who, when you were a sinner, he sent his Son Jesus to do something for you that you couldn't do for yourself, and you certainly didn't deserve it? Will you be the one to give him some praise right in the middle of chapter 6 of this book? (Insert your praise break here)

Will you be the one, not just with God… but with others that impact you? Will you be the one to stop and write a thank-you note to express gratitude to someone in your life? Every week, I write around twenty thank-you notes to people that do something amazing at our church or give for the first time. Hardly anyone handwrites anything nowadays. We just text, email, and send each other emojis and memes. So when someone takes the time to handwrite something, it stands out. I personally write these cards myself. I could delegate it, but it keeps me humble, connected, and I pray for those people. Some things you shouldn't delegate.

Will you be the parent that says thank you to the teacher over your children at your church and tell them, "Thank you for investing in my kids and serving my family and me!"? Will you be the one to stop and say thank you to a coach, teacher, or the person that led your small group? Will you stop and show honor and gratitude to your parents, pastors, spiritual leaders, or bosses? Or will you be like most people and say, "I don't have time to say thank you. I'm busy. I deserve what I have. I worked hard." Or will you be the one? Some of you might say, "I'm generally grateful. I'm good." If we're honest and put the spotlight on ourselves, we all have some work to do in this area.

TWO SONS WITH ENTITLED FRAMES

Let me quickly show you another interesting story from the New Testament. Jesus told this story about a guy who had two sons, and you can see the entitled frames in both of their lives. Two major phrases pop out from this mindset. The first one is, "I want it NOW!" I was recently in the drive-thru at a fast food place, and there was nothing fast about it. I found myself getting really frustrated until I pulled out of the line and left. I was mad and said, "I'm taking my business somewhere else! Ya'll need to get your act together! My car hasn't moved an inch in five minutes." I went to another spot and literally had to get out of my car and go inside to order. It was so inconvenient as I was trying to hurry to get back and finish writing this book. We've been so conditioned that we deserve, demand, and want it now!

You can see this same attitude in the younger son in this story known as "the Prodigal Son." Jesus says this in Luke 15:11, "A man had two sons. The younger son told his father, 'I want my share of your estate now before you die!'" I want it NOW! Traditionally, you receive your inheritance after someone dies. You get the life insurance after they pass away. That's the way it works, but this guy is like, I WANT IT NOW! I want to go live my life now. I don't want to wait. I don't want your rules. I want it right now! He was entitled. The father gave it to him. The Bible says this young guy left and squandered the money. He took a private jet to Vegas with his squad. He booked a penthouse on the strip. Every day consisted of gambling, drinking, and throwing parties. He hit the high-end boutiques to buy expensive clothes, shoes, and jewelry. When he pulled up in his Lambo, he was turning heads with his entourage. Everybody wanted to hang with him as he was buying drinks for the whole club. He would make it rain hundred-dollar bills from the balcony. Soon his account started running low. He got kicked out of the penthouse. He was at the pawn shop selling his jewelry. His friends left and went home, and his new friends disappeared. What his father took a lifetime to accumulate, the ungrateful son wasted in a matter of weeks. I want it now!

WHAT HIS FATHER TOOK A LIFETIME TO ACCUMULATE
THE UNGRATEFUL SON WASTED IN A MATTER OF WEEKS

What's interesting is that the upcoming generation have these "I want it now" frames. People in their twenties feel they deserve to live at the same standards of their parents, but they are half their age. They want the same kind of home, car, and vacations. It's easy to label them as a messed-up generation, but hold up, where did they learn it from? They learned it from their parents who thought, "If I want it, I'm going to get it now! I have this piece of plastic, and I can just charge it."

For generations, our society has been living beyond its means. We want it now, but our grandparents or great grandparents had this crazy philosophy. I'll try to explain it. It's kind of complicated and hard to understand, but I'll try to break it down as simply as I can. They believed this bizarre thing that if you wanted to buy something, you had to save up for it and buy it with money you actually had! I know that's super complex, so let me say it like this; If you don't have the money, you don't buy it. I know it sounds weird, right? Today, we just charge it and pay 24.9-percent interest on it for the rest of our lives. The thing that we charged on our card wore out, got lost, or outdated, but we got it when we wanted it, though!

The second major phrase that pops out with ungrateful frames is "I deserve MORE!" This was what the older brother was screaming in the story in Luke 15. The younger brother went and blew it all and ended up homeless. Then a recession hit, and there was a famine in the land. There were no good jobs available, so he ended up working in a pig pen. The Bible says he ate their food as there was nothing else to eat. There's a cultural context that makes this even deeper. Jewish people didn't eat pork. They didn't even touch it. It was considered unclean. Working with pigs was shameful. It was for Gentiles. He was super desperate to stoop to this kind of work. This is where he was humbled enough to go home and apologize to his father and ask to work as a servant. So he hitchhiked back home and arrived on his street. His clothes were worn out and dirty. He hadn't taken a shower in weeks. His father was sitting on the front porch and saw him walking up the sidewalk. He ran to meet him and hugged and kissed him. The son started apologizing and had his speech ready, but his dad cut him off and yelled, "My son who was lost is now found! My son who was dead is now alive! Let's throw a big welcome home party! Invite everyone! We're going to celebrate!"

This is a picture of our heavenly father who is waiting with open arms for his children when they spiritually come back home. Some of you reading this have been distant from God for a minute. You may have been wearing the "I want it now" frames, and you stepped away from God's plan as you were impatient, but you found yourself in a dark place and wanted to come back home and make things right, but you've been embarrassed, ashamed, and wondering if you'd be welcomed back. Luke 15 paints a clear picture that your heavenly father loves you and will welcome you back into the family.

This is a beautiful story that can bring a tear to your eye, the reunion of the lost son coming home, asking for forgiveness, and being received. Then the needle slides across the record... The older brother is like, "Wait, what? This dude goes and blows all your money and comes home broke and busted, and he gets a party? I've been here holding it down, doing the right thing, and nobody threw me a party. I DESERVE MORE!" If I try to put myself in his shoes, at first, I can kind of see his point, but look what his father told him. "Look, dear son, you have always stayed by me, and everything I have is yours." The older son who did the right thing had everything. He had access to his father and everything that was his. He also had his full inheritance still waiting. The younger brother wasted his and, of course, there would be some consequences he had to face for the rest of his life. The older brother still had everything, but copped an attitude that he wanted more.

HOW MUCH IS ENOUGH?

Many times we're blessed in so many ways, but we still want more. Our frames make us think that it's not enough. We can be pessimistic about our position. We're blinded to our blessings. Our tainted view causes us to fall into temptation. Our human nature makes us feel hopeless. Our greed keeps us from greatness. (You see what I did there? It's the chapter titles remixed.) Here's what we hear so often: I deserve a better-paying job, I deserve better benefits, and I deserve a better vacation. It's crazy that we have ten-year-olds crying because they don't have the latest iPhone with the best camera. Entitled frames are one of the nine, not the one. Will you be the one?

I want to help you put on some grateful frames, so let's take a moment and see what God would say to us about any ungratefulness in our hearts. Let's deal with it. We're going to ask a couple of questions. Ask God to expose any material ungratefulness in your life. Let me give you an example from my own life. It's really easy nowadays to get dissatisfied with your TV. When we first moved into our new house several years ago, we got rid of our big projection TV. Remember televisions with the huge backs on them? It was cutting edge technology when we first purchased it, but after thirteen years, it was so 2001. We didn't have any TV for the first few months, and then we got our very first flat screen for our bedroom. It was a forty-two-inch smart TV that blew our minds, but we were saving up for a bigger flat screen in the living room. Eventually, a friend of mine blessed us with a sixty-five-inch curved HDTV. Wow! That thing was next level, but now they have eighty-inch TVs for under $1,000, and suddenly my sixty-five-inch feels really small. I can barely see it. Maybe my eyes are getting worse as I get older. Of course, it was massive when I went from the forty-two-inch in my bedroom up to a sixty-five-inch, but it feels like it shrunk now, or we don't have the right kind of countertops, or we walk into our closet full of clothes and say, "I have nothing to wear." Say it: wear! Think about it. What have you complained about and been ungrateful about lately? It might be wishing you had a better job, a better car, a bigger house, better vacations... if that's you, own it.

Next, we need to ask God to expose any relational ungratefulness. You might be sick and tired of your parents being in your business. At least you have parents that actually care. Or it could be your husband. You might wish he made more money, be a better spiritual leader, or would learn to fix things around the house. Or it might be your wife. You wish she was more fun, more romantically involved, or she'd make food more often so you wouldn't spend so much money eating out. Or maybe you aren't happy because you don't have a boyfriend, girlfriend, or fiancée like everyone does. I could go on and on about the relationship comparisons we make, but I guarantee there are good things you could point out about some of the relationships you have right now. We don't focus on the positive if we aren't wearing our grateful frames. If you are relationally ungrateful, be honest.

The last question is to ask God to expose any circumstantial ungratefulness. I don't like my job, I don't like my hair, I don't like my lack of hair. I never get a break. I'm always catching Ls. I could go on and on, but you get it by now. Okay, we admit we all have some issues, and we all have some work to do. So where can I get a pair of those grateful frames, and how much do they cost? How do we create an attitude of gratitude? Decide to turn blessings into praise. Make a decision that every blessing God gives you, turn it into praise! This takes some work, but trust me, it's possible.

There were previous seasons of my life where I would have a pity party and focus on the negative. That gets old and depressing. Instead, I've now trained my mind to be optimistic and praise God for the good things he's doing in my life. I regularly come home with a list of blessings to share with my wife. She calls me the good news machine.

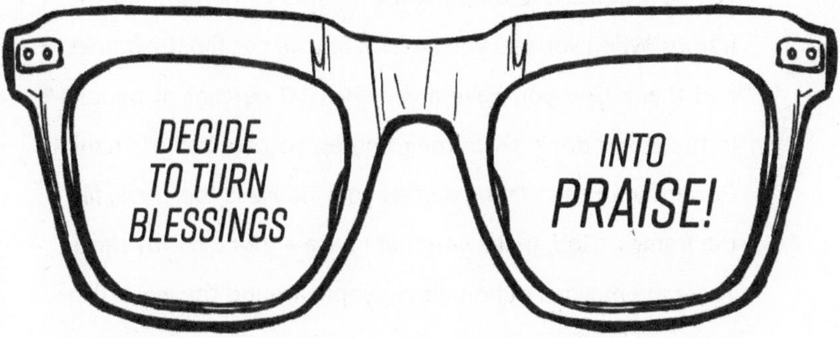
DECIDE TO TURN BLESSINGS
INTO PRAISE!

Every blessing I don't turn back to praise turns into pride. Pride wells up when blessing comes, and you take credit for it! "Look at what I did. I deserve this. I'm worthy of this." That is pride and entitlement. Instead, we flip the frames and say, "Every good thing comes from God! He is the giver of all good gifts. I will pause and praise and honor Him." This cultivates an attitude of gratitude. I love the way my guy Paul breaks it down in Philippians 4:11, "I have learned to be content with whatever I have. I know how to live on almost nothing or with everything. I have learned the secret of living in every situation whether it is with a full stomach or empty, with plenty or little. I can do everything through Christ who gives me strength." Let's go! If I'm healthy, or I'm not, If I have a lot of money, or I'm broke, If I like my job, or I don't, whatever the situation, I have learned to be content. I can do anything through Christ who gives me strength!

So when those ungrateful thoughts come in… flip the frames. When you feel you are sick of your car, flip the frames and thank God you have a car. Over 90 percent of people in the world don't. From their frames, you are ballin'! Thank God for your car. When you feel your house is too small, flip the frames. "God, thank you that I have a roof over my head. There are millions of homeless people around the world. I'm grateful I have air conditioning, a toilet, and running water." When you feel you are sick of your job, flip the frames. Thank God that you have stable income. Thank God for your co-workers, even though some of them might be difficult. God has placed you there on a mission to be a light and serve them. When you start feeling that you don't like your body, flip the frames. Thank God you're healthy. There are millions of people that died around the world in the pandemic, and you are still here. You made it. God has a plan and purpose for your life. Be grateful. The best is yet to come.

REFRAME IT:

1. What are some ways you've been entitled?
2. Which son do you most relate to from Luke 15? The prodigal who left and came home, or the one who stayed at home? Why?
3. What are some ways you need to flip the frames to become more grateful?

Watch the Frames Masterclass - Part 6
Log in at *www.tranzlationleadership.com*
and the course will be in your library if you followed the directions at the end of chapter 1.

7

LUSTFUL FRAMES VS PURE FRAMES

BEST SELLERS

These frames have been bestsellers throughout the history of mankind. Men and women have lusted for power, position, and possessions, but one of the biggest areas of lust we have struggled with is sexually. SEX can be treated as a dirty word around church, and it's rarely talked about, but, wait—who created sex? God did! He designed it, and our culture redefined it. This is where the lustful frames come into view. Most people are getting their sexual perspective through the lustful frames of media. This can lead us down the path to pornography, which is lustful frames on steroids. fightthenewdrug.org states that there are tens of billions of visits to the top porn websites. As people spend more time looking at the easy access of screens, the amount of porn being consumed continues to rise each year. It's safe to say that lustful frames are at an all-time high.

A few years back, I dropped a song entitled "Temptation" that talked about this epidemic:

Verse One:

Peep the culture's mentality/ Saturated by sexuality / Attracted by sensuality / Fantasizing a false reality / Here's the technicality / We're trying to fill a spot that's created for spirituality / It's grown to epic proportions / It's turned a beautiful thing into an ugly contortion / Take caution / When you browsing on the web late nights / Cuz there's over 300 million porn sites / It all starts with small bites / But beware—your appetite can grow / statistics will show / It's an epidemic that over 50 million Americans now know / Cuz they're addicted / They can't evict it / It's wrecked their expectations—they're afflicted / It's big business / Bigger than all pro sports put together / $12 billion dollars (Watch out!)—Temptation is clever!

Verse Two:

Sex sells and the culture buys / From music to cars to French fries / Legs, breasts, and thighs / Marinating in your thoughts—it ain't wise / From Tims and jeans—to suits and ties / It all starts with the eyes / For the girls . . . and especially for the guys / Lust entices with the tantal - eyes / It's no surprise / We try to take something that ain't ours—we plagiar - eyes / In our minds we try to reshape reality—we love to custom - eyes / But the result we despise / The consequences come and wreck us with the vandal - eyes / Don't fall for the lies / Don't fall for the disguise / Let's stand up together and rise / And open our spiritual eyes / See the truth—see the proof—Let's unite and mobile - eyes!

—Urban D. "Temptation" from the Un.orthodox album

SEXUAL SHIFTS

We live in a world that has had a huge sexual shift the past few years. In 2014, for the first time in American history, there were more unmarried adults than there were married adults. People are waiting longer to get married. They are staying single or just living together with someone. Culturally, we've seen sex becoming more and more casual. In 2015, same-sex marriage was nationally legalized. In 2016, several laws were passed, and legal battles took place about transgender bathrooms and discrimination against the LGBT community. In 2017–2018, the #MeToo movement exploded, where people began to publicly share about how they were sexually abused or taken advantage of by others. In the past few years, there have been multiple court battles about transgender men competing in women's sports and vice versa. That's just a small snapshot of the sexual shift of how things have rapidly changed in the past ten years. Our culture has all kinds of ideas on sexuality.

THE BEST SEX EVER

This chapter is about to get real. It's PG-13. Most people would like to have the best sex ever, but if you asked how that happens, you would get a lot of different answers. Let's start by looking at the Scripture and look at the design of our

Creator. If we look at the very beginning of the Bible, it says we were made in the imago Dei. That means the image of God. That is the foundation of our identity. Each one of us matters, we're significant, and we have a purpose! Unfortunately, not everyone is treated equally in our world. People judge you on your skin color, possessions, age, gender, and sexuality. Our culture puts labels on us and, many times, we let those labels define us. Those labels can be different than how God defines us. In the past decade, sexual labels have become a big deal; heterosexual, homosexual, transgender, bi-sexual, lesbian, gay, questioning, and asexual. There is also a group that is into artificial intelligence and robots. Yeah, that's a real thing, and it's going to grow in the future as technology advances. The culture puts people into those categories. We put people in those categories, and we put ourselves in those categories. You know what? The Bible doesn't do that. God doesn't do that. We are all in the same category. We are sexual beings. We have sexual desires. Some of those desires are in God's design, and some are outside of God's design. It doesn't make up our identity.

OUR IDENTITY STARTS IN THE FACT
THAT WE'RE MADE IN GOD'S IMAGE

Our identity from a biblical perspective is much deeper than that. We're made in God's image, and he deeply loves each one of us. Ever since Adam and Eve messed up, we all have this sin nature that God wants to redeem, and that's why he sent Jesus. Our identity starts in the fact that we're made in God's image. My identity is not my sexual desires. Sex is a great thing, but it's not essential for us living a full life. There are a lot of people that lived full lives and remained celibate. Look at Jesus! That's not everyone's calling. It wasn't mine (thank you, Lord!). My wife and I recently celebrated twenty-five years of marriage. I love her more than ever! Lucy and I remained celibate until our wedding day. That may sound crazy or old school in today's culture. Honestly, it was really challenging! We loved each other, we were young, and hormones were on ten, but I'm letting you know it's possible with God's help. We're grateful we waited, and we have no regrets. We know it's one of the things that has helped our marriage stay strong. We honored God's blueprint. Side note: I had this fear that I was going to die before my wedding night or maybe on our wedding day, Jesus would come back, and I'd hear the trumpets and be like, "NO, Jesus, not yet—give me a few more minutes."

HIS FORMULA

God doesn't put us into these categories of heterosexual,

bi-sexual, or homosexual; we are just sexual beings. So if that's true, then as sexual beings, what is God's design for sex? What is his formula? He made it and created it to be good. He designed it for procreation and recreation, aka procreation and pleasure. So what are the requirements for his plan for sex? The Bible isn't ambiguous about this subject. There are some subjects that the Bible isn't as clear on, like should you be team Apple or team Android? I think real Christians are on team Apple, but I can't biblically prove it! On the subject of sexuality, the Bible is pretty clear. All the way from the beginning of the book of Genesis, when God creates humanity, he introduces this thing called marriage. In Genesis 2:24, the Bible says, "This explains why a man leaves his father and mother and is joined to his wife and the two are united into one through sexual union." So sex is to be enjoyed in the context of marriage, which is a covenant. The Bible defines that between a man and woman. The Bible is consistent with that. It never varies from that. Anything outside of that is outside of God's design. It can be sinful and damaging. Listen, I know that's not popular, not what's trending, and not considered progressive, but it's the Creator's design. It's his formula.

Many of you reading this would say you have a relationship with Christ. Some of you might not be there yet, but I'm so glad you are here reading these words. For those of us who have said yes to Jesus, we strive to be like him and follow his teachings that we find in the Scripture. So what did Jesus say about same-sex marriage? Actually, he said nothing. It never came up. It was never directly addressed. Why? Because history shows us that it wasn't a public issue in culture at that time, so there was no reason to bring it up. We can see Jesus talking about marriage in Matthew 19:4–6, where he was asked a question about marriage, and he said this, "'Haven't you read the scriptures?' Jesus replied. 'They record that from the beginning God made them male and female.'" And then he quoted Scripture from Genesis 2, "This is why a man leaves his father and mother and is joined to his wife and the two are united into one. Since they are no longer two, but one, let no one split apart what God has joined together." So as Christians, we should affirm what Jesus said, even if we might not fully understand it right away or not like it at first. It's a trust that we know he loves us and has our best interest in mind.

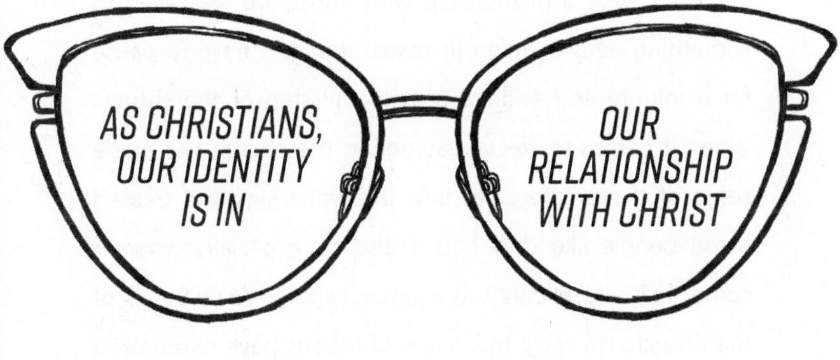
AS CHRISTIANS,
OUR IDENTITY
IS IN
OUR
RELATIONSHIP
WITH CHRIST

As Christians, our identity is in our relationship with Christ. Culture tells us that our identity is in our desires. Culture encourages us to wear our lustful frames and do whatever we want: sleep around with lots of people, have fun, and just use protection. Culture encourages us to be involved with same-sex relationships. It's all good. It's popular. It's trending, especially with the younger generations. My daughter was attending a Christian high school a few years ago, and every girl at her lunch table was suddenly into dating girls. They were pressuring her to admit that she also was into it, but she didn't. Culture used to tell us porn was good, and it was normal. Now, it's really fascinating that since the #MeToo movement jumped off, there have been lots of research coming out that shows how dangerous porn can be. There are now mainstream movements and campaigns against porn. Wow. . . really? Many Christians have been warning people about this for decades, and we were considered outdated and crazy.

If we have a relationship with Christ, we are called to something deeper than our sexual desires. I have to pause for a minute and address a major misstep of the church. When it comes to sexual categories, the church has made some of those categories into the worst sins and treated those people like they had a disease, especially when it comes to homosexuality. As a pastor, I apologize on behalf of the Church. I'm sorry that some Christians have demonized people that have a certain sexual orientation and made them out to be worse sinners than other sinners. That's not right. That's not how true Christians should treat people. That's not how we have ever rolled at our church. We have always accepted everyone at our church and welcomed them and showed them the love of Christ. Just because we accept someone doesn't mean we approve of his or her lifestyle. As he or she hears the truth shared in love and builds a relationship with Christ and with others, it creates opportunities for conversations about every area of his or her life. At the end of the day, the Holy Spirit is the one that has to convict his or her heart and help him or her see the truth.

I encourage you to read 1 Corinthians 5–7. Paul is the one who wrote it and talks about sexual sin in a way that is equal. He breaks down several different scenarios. The Corinthians were some ratchet people. They were wild! At the beginning of chapter 5, he is correcting them because there was a man in the church that was sleeping with his stepmother. Everybody knew about it, but nobody was saying anything. Paul was instructing them, saying, "Yo! This type of behavior can't become normal and accepted; it's not cool!" Read it! It's in there, and it gets real! In chapter 6, the conversation continues, and Paul warns them that people who continue to live in a lifestyle of sin won't share in the kingdom of God. Look at what he breaks down in verse 9:

I wrote you in my earlier letter that you shouldn't make yourselves at home among the sexually promiscuous. I didn't mean that you should have nothing at all to do with outsiders of that sort. Or with crooks, whether blue or white collar. Or with spiritual phonies, for that matter. You'd have to leave the world entirely to do that! But I am saying that you shouldn't act as if everything is just fine when a friend who claims to be a Christian is promiscuous or crooked, is flip with God or rude to friends, get drunk or becomes greedy or predatory. You can't just go along with this, treating it as acceptable behavior. I'm not responsible for what the outsiders do, but don't we have some responsibility for those within our community of believers? God decides on the outside, but we need to decide when our brothers and sisters are out of line and if necessary clean house.

The Bible makes it crystal clear that we are called to hold each other accountable when we have lustful sinful frames. Of course, we are called to do this with wisdom and in love. We have to look out for one another. This is what real relationships do. We need people in our corner to help us stay on track.

7

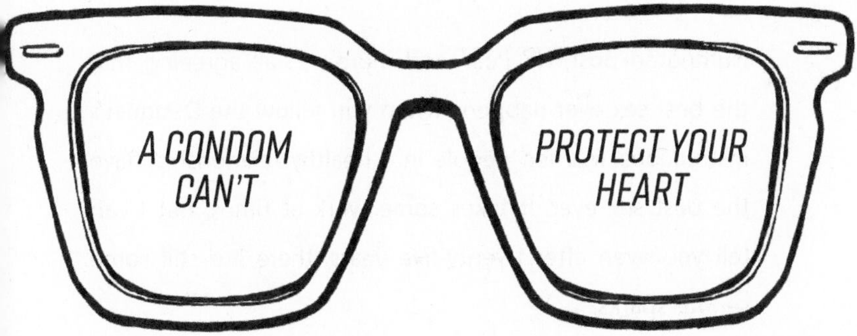
A CONDOM CAN'T
PROTECT YOUR HEART

We all get tempted. Sexual sin is about behavior, not about orientation, desire, or temptation. We are all temped in many ways; some of us with greed, pride, envy, anger, or sexually. We are weaker in some of these areas more than others. Jesus himself was tempted. Temptation itself is not sin. It only becomes a sin when a person yields to that temptation and engages in sinful behavior and attitude. So what is the formula for the best sex ever without lustful frames? What does it look like? How do I achieve it? We follow the designer's instructions. It's between a man and woman in the covenant of marriage. When we go outside of that, there can be pain, regrets, shame, broken hearts, and even physical effects, like sexually transmitted diseases. A condom can't protect your heart! When you are in a healthy marriage, you are not worried about trust with your spouse. You can fully be yourself and have the best sex ever. There is freedom in the marriage bedroom to have fun and meet each other's needs. Research shows that married people have the best sex and the most sex. Google that. There are articles from Cosmopolitan,

Huffington post, NY Post, and more . . . all agreeing that the best sex ever happens when you follow the Designer's instructions. Married people in a healthy relationship have the best sex ever. It takes some work at times, but I can tell you even after twenty-five years, there are still some serious sparks.

BORN THIS WAY

People are all born a certain way. We're born into sin. Our sinful nature attracts us to the wrong frames. For some, it might be lying, lust, alcohol, same-sex attraction, pills, or greed, but we're all born with this sin nature that pulls us toward the frames that aren't our Designer's brand. Whatever your struggles are sexually, God can change and transform you, and the culture has lied to us and sang catchy songs telling us we can't change even if we want to... even if we tried. The truth is that nothing is impossible with God. I know lots of people who have overcome sexual sin and lustful frames.

We laid out God's formula for the best sex ever, but what if you are single or in a struggling marriage? This is where the battle is most intense. God created us as sexual beings, and when there is no sex in our picture, it can heighten our senses and emotions. We can get easily triggered when we see things on our screens or certain situations in real life. This is where prayer, boundaries, discipline, and intentionality are needed. You must have a consistent prayer life, where you are being honest with God and bringing this before him. You have to be honest with yourselves and those you are accountable with. It's important to set up realistic boundaries. There is a single guy from my church who finishes all of his text messages and social media posts in his car before he walks into his apartment each night. When he walks inside, he puts his phone in a drawer for the night. Why? Because he got strategic and set up a boundary. He was most tempted at night while scrolling on his phone and would regularly end up looking at porn. Boundaries are nothing unless we follow them and stay disciplined. You need people to hold you accountable. This is crazy; as I was typing this very paragraph, that same guy I'm telling you about texted me. I asked him how he was doing in that area and told him I was including it in my book. We have to be brutally honest with ourselves about our weaknesses. We need people in our lives who we can be accountable to and share our struggles and our wins.

As a pastor, I know there are so many people who have been fighting a losing battle with lustful frames for years. Some have given up. I want to encourage you today that victory is possible! Many of you are very strategic and intentional with your job, art, family, children, and ___________(Fill in the blank), but many times, we get lazy with our frames and don't have a solid plan to purify them. If you fail to plan, you can plan to fail.

THIS WASN'T SUPPOSED TO BE INCLUDED!

This chapter wasn't supposed to be in the book. I had already sent the manuscript to the editor. I felt something was still missing in these pages. God started speaking to me to add the chapter about lustful frames. Many Christians and churches don't talk enough about these frames that are wrecking so many lives. It's tearing apart marriages and families. It's destroying ministries. There are weapons and resources to fight this battle. You are not alone. The book, Every Man's Battle and Every Woman's Battle are great tools we have used at our church multiple times. There is accountability software you can also install on your devices if necessary. This chapter is in here for you to take action today! Work on a plan and get some trusted friends involved. We pray that you'll yield to God's Spirit and know that God has more for you, and with his power, you can change these frames and reach the full potential he has for you.

REFRAME IT:

1. Have you struggled with lustful frames recently?
2. What are your trigger points that cause you to put lustful frames on?
3. What is your plan to purify your frames?

Watch the Frames Masterclass - Part 7
Log in at *www.tranzlationleadership.com*
and the course will be in your library if you followed the directions at the end of chapter 1.

TEMP FRAMES VS ETERNAL FRAMES

EXPIRATION

Most frames will last on average from one to three years. They eventually wear out. They are temporary. The prescription for the lenses are only valid for one to two years. Once it expires, people must get a new one in order to get new frames. This is necessary as the optometrist needs to examine your eyes and check for vision changes. The frames you are wearing today are temporary for this season of your life. Prescriptions will change, perspectives will change, and preferences will change. Expiration is inevitable.

Back in the early nineties, I started wearing my very first pair of frames. They were small circle wire frames that every cool R&B singer was rocking. My young eyes were still 20/20, so the lenses were clear. I didn't need to wear frames, but it was all about the look. Soon the fad faded, and I was back to wearing no frames at all. Around 2009, the thick frames on the side with the small boxy lenses were in style. I saw a dope pair of Ferrari frames at the flea market for ten dollars.

I bought them for fun and wore them that Sunday to church. I preached in them and got dozens of positive comments. Everyone thought they were real in both ways. They thought I really needed glasses, but they were just clear lenses. They also thought they were real Ferrari frames, which I didn't even know was a thing. Apparently, my pair was just a bootleg version. A few months later, I accidentally sat on the frames, they bent and were crooked. They were a throw-away pair.

There are so many things in life that we give our full attention to as if they are going to last forever. The Bible helps us reframe this in 2 Corinthians 4:18, "So we don't look at the troubles we can see now; rather, we fix our gaze on things that cannot be seen. For the things we see now will soon be gone, but the things we cannot see will last forever." I had to learn this lesson the hard way with my very first car. I saved up and worked hard for that car. I paid cash, but it was already nine years old when I purchased it. It was in decent condition as it only had one owner, but there were a lot of things I wanted to upgrade on it. So the next few years, I put all of my extra money into transforming this Chevy Cavalier into a wannabe sports car low rider. I painted it (twice), got rims, wide tires, lowered it, tinted the windows, installed a detachable face CD player, ten-inch subs with an amplifier, seat covers, new car mats, air fresheners, a long mirror all the way across, and to top it all off, I got purple neon lights underneath. Yeah, I went all out! I put more money into the car than it was worth.

Adding these bells and whistles while living in the city made my car a target. It was broken into, and my sound system was stolen. Then a few months later, the entire car was stolen and had major damage. I got it back and still fixed it back up. It was my baby. I had invested so much into it. Then another sound system was stolen (the third one), and I finally realized this vicious cycle I put myself in. I had been putting so much focus on this temporary thing I couldn't even keep safe. The car's value kept going down as it was getting older and had more and more issues. It had an expiration date! I flipped my frames and began to focus on things that would last forever.

IT HITS DIFFERENT

Now that I'm in my forties, things hit different. I recently realized that I probably have more life behind me than I have in front of me. That's a sobering thought. My daughters are teenagers, and they are growing up so quickly. I regularly look at pictures from just a few years ago when they were younger. Those days flew by so fast! My wife and I recently celebrated twenty-five years of marriage and twenty-five years of ministry at Crossover Church. Maybe I have another ten to fifteen years to serve as the lead pastor, but I'm realizing how temporary everything is. At some point in the future, I'll be passing the baton to the next generation. I'm trying to maximize every moment and every move.

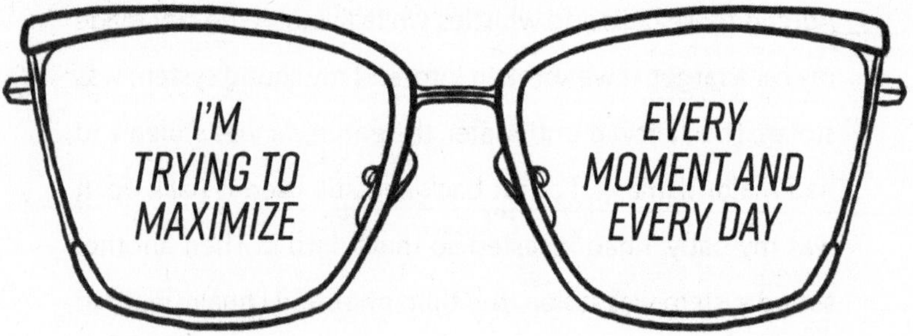

I'M TRYING TO MAXIMIZE
EVERY MOMENT AND EVERY DAY

2017 was a tough year for my family. In January, my father passed away after sixteen years of sickness that started from a brain aneurism and stroke. My mother had been fighting cancer for a few years, and eight months later, she also passed. In addition, one of my spiritual fathers who was the head elder at our church went home to be with the Lord. It was a lot of loss in a short time period. As we celebrated their lives, told stories, and looked at pictures, it was another sobering reminder of how temporary our time is here.

When you become "an adult," you are supposed to start planning for retirement. Most people don't always start thinking about this until they start to get a little older, but eventually, it's on your radar. They tell us we should save up and get ready. I definitely agree with this, but what I don't agree with is how our culture pushes that the goal is to just retire. We are called to be productive and flourish, even in our sixties, seventies, and beyond. We might retire from our primary career, but God can still use us in each season to have an eternal impact. I've watched so many people save up, invest, and work so hard to retire at sixty-five, and then they die in just a few short months or years. Many people I know never even make it to retirement. They never were able to enjoy what they saved up for. My father got sick at fifty-five. I'm not trying to be depressing, but my point is if all you are thinking about is retirement, you have temporary frames on. Retirement season is just a few years in the last chapter of your life. We should be praying and planning with eternal frames on.

A few years ago, I heard about someone who was working on their 500-year plan. Wait, what? They were mapping out their company, foundation, and endowments for their family for several generations to come. They wanted to make sure their legacy lasted and had an eternal impact beyond just a few years after they passed away. They were putting standards, ministry initiatives, and boundaries in place to ensure things would run according to their wishes. My mind was blown. Because most of us have temporary frames on, we probably never think about having impact hundreds of years from now. I pray that the influence of my writing, teaching, music, and art will outlive me.

My parents passing away made me really focus on legacy. I heard that word, studied that word and even preached about that word many times. It hit different now as I realized the generation that made me was now gone. I'm living their legacy, and my kids will soon be mine and theirs when I'm gone. As my sister Tammy and I cleaned out my parents' house, we found all of my father's notebooks in the back of the closet.

My dad was a pastor for over thirty years before he got sick. He had stacks of these yellow-lined notebooks where he wrote scriptures and sermon notes. My father had this amazing handwriting script that looked like a fancy font. He loved to use highlighters of all different colors in his Bibles and lined notebooks. I remember waking up to use the bathroom at 4:30 a.m., and my father would already be awake sitting at the kitchen table with his Bible open and his notebooks and markers. I also remember his life was much more than just studying the Scripture; he made it his mission to apply it. He loved people and visited dozens of homes each month. When I was younger, he regularly took me to visit shut-ins and church members as he prayed with them, offered communion, and shared a meal. He loved to eat and laugh with his people. He made them feel like family. My pops left a rich legacy that eternally impacted so many people at the five different congregations he pastored over the years. That's legacy.

My hope is that as you finish this book, some of the principles you read about will change your perspective forever. I pray you'll move from pessimistic to optimistic. I pray that your blind spots will be illuminated with a fresh new vision. I pray any areas of tainted vision will be wiped clean to see with clarity. I pray that your human nature will be on the journey to be transformed to become more and more like Christ. I pray that you'll eliminate any greed in your life and replace it with more generosity. I pray that you'll recognize any entitlement that we all struggle with, and you'll develop a new attitude of gratitude. Lastly, I pray that we'll all move from looking through temporary frames to see things from an eternal perspective. If you change your frames, you can change the game.

REFRAME IT:

1. What is an example of how you looked at a situation with temporary frames?
2. Have you lost any family or friends that has made you think about legacy?
3. What could a 100, 250, and 500-year plan look like for your family, company, or foundation after you are gone?

Watch the Frames Masterclass - Part 8
Log in at *www.tranzlationleadership.com*
and the course will be in your library if you followed the directions at the end of chapter 1.

CHECK OUT

URBAN D'S MUSIC

ON ALL PLATFORMS!

MUSIC Spotify iTunes

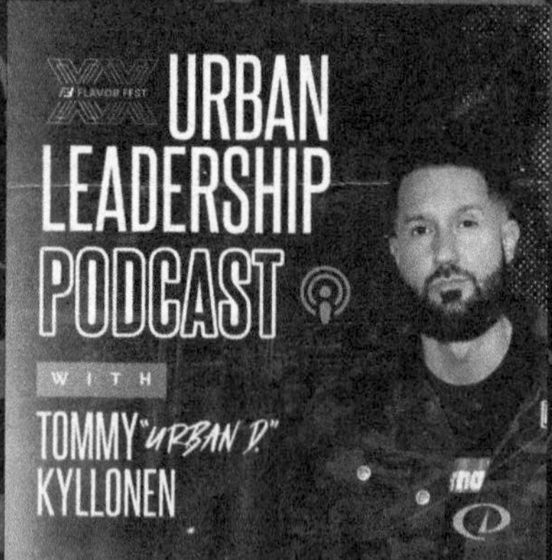

ALSO CHECK OUT

Pastor Tommy's Podcast

FLAVOR FEST

URBAN LEADERSHIP PODCAST on

www.youtube.com/urband813

and all podcast platforms!

ABOUT THE AUTHOR

Tommy "Urban D." Kyllonen has dedicated his life to serve his church, his city, and you, as a pastor, Hip-Hop artist, author, entrepreneur and philanthropist.

For over 20 years Tommy has served as lead pastor at Crossover Church in beautiful Tampa, Florida. It's a blend of multi-ethnic, multi-generational, multi-class community. This led Crossover to be recognized as an example for other churches to model after, while also experiencing over 30x growth under Tommys leadership. Crossover is located in a 43,000 square foot facility (formerly a Toys R' Us) in Tampa's Uptown District. *Outreach Magazine* recognized Crossover as one of America's most innovative churches and has also been featured in USA Today, Newsweek, CBS News, BET News and several regional media outlets.

Follow Tommy on all social media platforms ***@urband813***

Urban D. is an internationally known Hip-Hop artist that has released nine albums and several remix projects. He has performed and spoken at concerts and conferences across the U.S. as well as overseas in Japan, Australia, The UK, Germany, and Nigeria.

Tommy has authored six books. His most acclaimed book *Love Our City* is a 30-day devotional format for churches and small groups to go through together with a video based curriculum. It also includes a community service project aspect. His church has used this to reach thousands of new people. They created a leaders box kit that gives churches all the tools to launch Love Our City in their communities. Hundreds of churches have joined the Love Our City movement. Tommy is also the publisher of *S.O.U.L. MAG* magazine, which so far has produced 29 issues.

With a passion to see other leaders win, he founded the *Flavor Fest Urban Leadership Conference,* which has trained thousands of leaders since it's inception in 1999. Also, his Monthly Coaching Network has trained hundreds of pastors and church planters, and he is the chairman of the *Uptown Innovation Partnership* board, allowing him to serve as a connector / influencer in his city.

Tommy lives in Tampa, Florida with his wife Lucy and his two daughters, Deyana and Sophia.

FRAMES

YOUR FRAMES CAN **CHANGE THE GAME**

TOMMY *URBAN D.* KYLLONEN

FOREWORD BY **KEVIN *KB* BURGESS**

Tranzlation Leadership
TAMPA, FL